# SERIOUSLY SENIOR MOMENTS

# SERIOUSLY SENIOR MOMENTS

Or, Have You Bought This Book Before?

## Geoff Tibballs

Michael O'Mara Books Limited

First published in Great Britain in 2010 by
Michael O'Mara Books Limited
9 Lion Yard
Tremadoc Road
London SW4 7NQ

Papers used by Michael O'Mara Books Limited are natural, recyclable
products made from wood grown in sustainable forests. The manufacturing
processes conform to the environmental regulations of the country of origin.

A CIP catalogue record for this book is available from the British Library.

ISBN: 978-1-84317-488-2

3 5 7 9 10 8 6 4 2

www.mombooks.com

Text design and typesetting by Design 23
Illustrations by David Woodroffe

Printed in the UK by CPI Mackays, Chatham, ME5 8TD

# INTRODUCTION

How many times a week do you have to call your own mobile phone in order to find it? How often have you walked into a room, been momentarily distracted and then completely forgotten the purpose of your visit? And how often have you put important documents in such a safe place that you can never find them again? If you've ever got hold of the wrong end of the stick and then misplaced the stick entirely, you have fallen victim to a senior moment.

Don't be lulled into a false sense of security by the word 'senior'. These bouts of distraction, lapses in concentration and episodes of temporary absent-mindedness can occur at any age. You don't have to be over forty for your favourite phrase to be 'What was I doing?' or for your mind to wander so far that it is out of breath by the time it eventually returns to you. I had a senior moment at about sixteen when, in the process of eating a sweet, I kept the wrapper in my hand and threw the sweet into the fire (I'm senior enough to have grown up with coal fires). Furthermore, when I relayed this sad little tale to a school friend, she confessed that she had once done exactly the same thing. Of course, I may have had senior moments before then – but I've forgotten them.

I do, however, remember the first time I was on the receiving end of a senior moment. It was during the bitterly cold British winter of 1963, and the headmaster of our school decided, in an unprecedented act of compassion, to let us all go home early one afternoon because of the thick snow. The school had a system whereby a central buzzer was pressed to denote the end of each lesson, but unfortunately the headmaster, not being used to this apparatus, accidentally pressed the fire alarm instead.

Consequently instead of going home early, 500 boys were left shivering in the playground for half an hour while the red-faced headmaster explained that there was in fact no fire: he had simply had a senior moment.

There is a tendency to worry about having senior moments but, rather like that extra roast potato, the occasional one never does any harm. As this book shows, such great minds as Nelson Mandela, Einstein and Beethoven have all suffered from senior-momentitis at one time or another, and if it's good enough for them, then it's good enough for the rest of us.

The best thing to do is to have a good laugh about it, safe in the knowledge that whenever you forget a friend's name, try to make a phone call on the TV remote or struggle in vain to open a screw-top bottle of wine with a corkscrew, you're in good company.

GEOFF TIBBALLS, 2010

## GONE AND FORGOTTEN

American actress Mary Martin (mother of Larry Hagman) was still mourning the death of her second husband, Richard Halliday, when she went to see Dame Edith Evans's one-woman show at London's Theatre Royal in the 1970s. After the show, she went backstage to meet Dame Edith.

'Oh, Edith!' she wailed. 'Since I last saw you I've lost my dear husband!'

'I lost mine a long time ago,' replied Dame Edith matter-of-factly. 'I can't even remember his name.'

---

### MEMORY TEST

'By the time you're eighty years old you've learned everything. You only have to remember it.'

BILL VAUGHAN

---

## CLASSICAL GAS

John was sitting in a diner one lunchtime when he suddenly realized that he needed to break wind. The music was really loud, so he thought he could disguise his gas by timing his emissions to the beat of the music. After a couple of songs, he started to feel much better.

As he finished his coffee, however, he noticed that everybody in the diner was staring at him. That was when he remembered he was listening to his iPod …

## OH, CRUMBS!

The 1824 war between Britain and the Ashanti (part of present-day Ghana) saw the British troops fighting a desperate rearguard action. Surrounded by 10,000 warriors and running low on ammunition, as a last-ditch attempt at keeping the enemy at bay they ordered the army's stores manager, Charles Brandon, to break open the reserve ammunition that he had brought from the coast. With the Ashanti forces closing in fast, Brandon unscrewed the ammunition boxes, only to find that they contained biscuits instead. He had brought the wrong box.

## TREE TROUBLE

A State Trooper stopped a car on a quiet country road and approached the elderly driver.

'Excuse me, ma'am,' he said, 'but can you explain why you've been driving so erratically for the past five miles? You were weaving all over the road.'

'Thank heaven you're here, officer,' gasped the old lady. 'I very nearly had an accident. I looked up and there was this tree right in front of me. I swerved to the left and there was another tree. So I swerved to the right and there was yet another tree. It was the most frightening experience I've had in my whole life.'

The officer calmly reached through the side window to the rear-view mirror and said, 'Ma'am, there was no tree. It was your air freshener.'

## DOWN IN THE DUMPS

Cars would be so much simpler for us to handle if they didn't have so many knobs, pedals and sticky-out bits. It's bad enough when we accidentally switch on the windscreen wipers every time we intend to turn right but confusing the brake and the accelerator can be no laughing matter, as sixty-five-year-old Heiner Mollard found to his cost. Backing his car up to a garbage bunker at a Swiss recycling centre in 2010, Herr Mollard accidentally pressed the accelerator instead of the brake and plunged thirty feet over the edge and down into the pile of trash. After he had been winched to safety, he suffered the additional embarrassment of being fined $100 for leaving an 'inappropriate item' – his car – in a recycling bin.

## LIKE A BROTHER

Scriptwriter Barry Cryer was standing at the bar at ATV's Elstree Studios in the early 1970s with American director Barry Levinson when the latter pointed out the elderly Groucho Marx sitting in the restaurant. It so happened that Cryer had brought with him a copy of *The Groucho Letters* in the hope that the great man might sign it, and Levinson offered to take the book over.

Cryer watched apprehensively as Levinson spoke to Groucho, who then peered over to the bar to see who was making the request and, with a quivering hand, signed the title page. When the book was brought back to him, Cryer saw that it had simply been signed 'From Groucho'. He was perfectly happy with that but Levinson insisted that it should be personalized, so he took the book back to Groucho and asked him to write 'To Barry' and also to add 'Marx' after 'Groucho'.

This was where matters became confusing as Groucho wrote 'Marx' in the wrong place and was immediately corrected by Levinson. The result is that Barry Cryer now owns a copy of the book with the dedication: 'To Barry Marx from Groucho Marx'.

---

### SHORT FLIGHT

An old lady phoned British Airways and asked, 'Can you tell me how long it takes to fly from London to New York?'
'Just a minute, madam,' said the operator.
'Oh, that is quick,' said the old lady. And she hung up.

---

## UNSCHEDULED JOURNEY

Airports can be baffling places. There
are so many rules and regulations to
follow that it's no wonder some of us
occasionally get a little confused.
Checking in at Stockholm airport in
preparation for catching a flight to
Germany in 2008, a seventy-eight-
year-old woman misunderstood
instructions and placed herself instead
of her case on an unmanned baggage
belt. No sooner did she lie down on
the belt than she was automatically
swept off to the baggage handling
centre, where surprised staff helped
her get back on her feet. Happily she
was able to catch her flight as planned.

## MIND WENT BLANK

As Polish-born American pianist Josef Hofmann sat at his stool
and prepared himself for the start of a concert, an expectant
hush fell over the hall. For nigh on thirty seconds there was total
silence. Then, with a puzzled expression on his face, Hofmann
looked up from his piano and leaned over to speak to a lady in
the front row of the audience.

'Please may I see your programme, madam?' he whispered.
'I've forgotten what comes first!'

## HIDDEN MEANINGS

A sure sign of advancing years is that sometimes we say things without thinking them through properly. We know what we mean but it doesn't always come out quite the way we intended. I speak from personal experience. After relatives that we had not seen for some time came to stay for a week, my mother said to them as they left: 'Let's hope it won't be so long next time.' She meant their absence; my father and I interpreted it as meaning their stay.

If it's of any consolation, she was by no means alone, as the following examples show:

'And now a record dedication for Mrs Ethel Smith who is 100 years old today – but I'm told she's dead with-it.'
– BBC Radio 2 announcer David Bellan

'I think that gay marriage should be between a man and a woman.' – Arnold Schwarzenegger

'I believe that people would be alive today if there were a death penalty.' – Nancy Reagan

'A lot of actresses have complained that as they get older the parts dry up.' – Jimmy Young

'Ladies and gentlemen, now you can have a bikini for a ridiculous figure.' – US radio announcer

'Those who survived the San Francisco earthquake said, "Thank God, I'm still alive." But of course those who died, their lives will never be the same again.' – Barbara Boxer

'The snow came with a vengeance. I had a good eight inches last night.' – US weather girl

'We all have ancestors, and in this series I will encourage you to dig up yours.' – UK TV presenter

'Arnie Palmer, usually a great putter, seems to be having trouble with his long putts. However he has no trouble dropping his shorts.' – US golf commentator

'And don't forget, on Sunday, you can hear the two-minute silence on Radio 1.' – UK DJ Steve Wright

## GUESS THE AGE

Three mischievous old ladies were sitting on a bench outside a nursing home when an old man shuffled past.

They yelled to him, 'We bet we can tell exactly how old you are!'

'Impossible!' the old man scoffed.

'Sure we can,' said one of the women. 'Just drop your pants and we'll tell you your exact age.'

So the old man took off his clothes.

'Now spin around three times,' they commanded.

Reluctantly the old man spun around three times and nearly toppled over because it made him so giddy.

When he had finished, the women called out, 'You're eighty-eight years old.'

Standing with his pants around his ankles, the old man said, 'That's right. How in the world did you work that out?'

The women cackled.

'We were at your birthday party yesterday!'

## DOCTOR'S ORDERS

A man in his late fifties went to the doctor for his annual physical. He told the doctor, 'My memory is terrible these days. I forget where I live, I forget where I've parked my car, and I go into stores and can't remember what I want. And when I finally reach the checkout, I realize I've forgotten my wallet. It's driving me crazy, doc. What can I do?'

The doctor thought for a moment and said, 'Pay me in advance.'

---

### SOMETHING MISSING

Police detectives reported that a Californian counterfeiter had done a thoroughly professional job creating the forged notes that he handed over to a store owner. In fact, they said the only clue they had that the cash might not be genuine was that he had forgotten to print both sides of the dollar bills.

---

## THAT'S THE WORD!

The absent-mindedness of mathematics professor Norbert Wiener has provided a fund of anecdotes. One tells how he was sitting in the campus lounge at the Massachusetts Institute of Technology, intensely studying a paper on the table. Several times he stood up and paced around before returning to the paper, his face a picture of concentration. Everyone present was impressed by how obviously dedicated he was to his work. Then suddenly he stood up once more and this time collided with a student who responded with, 'Good afternoon, Professor Wiener.'

Wiener stopped in his tracks, stared in wonderment, clapped a hand to his forehead and declared, 'Wiener! That's the word!' He then ran back to the table to fill the word 'wiener' in the crossword puzzle that he was doing.

Then there was the time when he went to a conference and parked his car in the large lot. When the conference was over, he went to the lot but forgot where he had parked his car. He had also forgotten what his car looked like. So he waited until all the other cars were driven away and then took the one that was left.

On yet another occasion, Wiener drove over 100 miles to a mathematics conference at Yale University. By the end of the conference, he had completely forgotten that he had come by car and instead travelled home by bus. The next morning, he went out to his garage, saw that it was empty, and phoned the police to report that somebody had stolen his car while he had been away.

## NIGHT DUTY

George was in his late sixties so his wife was surprised to hear him suddenly ask one morning, 'How would you feel about trying for another baby?'

'You must be crazy!' she exclaimed. 'Have you forgotten about all those sleepless nights we used to have? We'd never cope with it at our age.'

'Sure, I know I used to complain about getting up at two o'clock in the morning to feed the baby,' he said, 'but it wouldn't be a problem any more.'

'Why not?' asked his wife.

'Because these days I usually have to get up around that time anyway.'

## EMERGENCY REPAIRS

Driving her husband's van, Angela could tell it wasn't going to be her lucky day when the vehicle's fan belt snapped on the highway. Resourceful as ever, she took off her tights and used one of the legs as a replacement belt. She hoped that this contraption would hold firm until she reached the nearest town, where she would be able to buy a proper fan belt.

Just a few miles down the road, however, the tights leg snapped. Undeterred, she pressed the other leg of her tights into service but that, too, lasted only a matter of minutes. She now bitterly regretted always buying cheap tights.

Still four miles from the nearest garage, there was only one thing for it. Crouching behind the van on the hard shoulder, she slipped off her knickers and, using them as a frilly fan belt, coaxed the vehicle gingerly into town. On finally reaching the sanctuary of the garage, she pulled into the forecourt, carefully climbed out of the van, opened the rear doors and under a pile of boxes spotted a toolkit … containing a spare fan belt.

## STOP ME IF YOU'VE HEARD IT

A comedian landed an afternoon booking at a retirement home. He found it hard to work up much enthusiasm for the gig so when his first joke went down really well with the elderly audience, he just told the same joke over and over again – twenty-five times in total.

At the end, an old man came up to him and said, 'I don't know how you remember them all.'

## MISTAKEN IDENTITY

Even the greatest of men are prone to occasional senior moments. Nelson Mandela was attending a charity event in 2010 when he mistook outspoken British TV presenter Jeremy Clarkson for an American astronaut. The mistake was perhaps understandable because Mandela was due to meet a group of astronauts later in the day, but in any case Clarkson could not bring himself to correct the legendary leader.

'It was tricky,' admitted the *Top Gear* presenter afterwards. 'I couldn't very well say that we weren't astronauts, as that might

look argumentative. Nor could I say that we made a poky BBC2 programme about cars – because then he might wonder what on earth we were doing wasting his valuable time. So I did what I thought best and pretended that I had visited the moon. I said it was very rocky and dusty and there was not much gravity.'

## CALENDAR CHAOS

Delighted to find love again at her time of life, a senior Maine lady excitedly informed everyone in town that she was getting married on the last day in September. But come the big day her joy turned to misery as she was left standing at the altar after the groom failed to show up. She finally tracked him down that evening and demanded an explanation.

'Why weren't you at the church this afternoon?' she cried. 'You made me look foolish in front of all my friends. How could you do this to me on our wedding day?'

The errant groom fell silent.

'Was *today* our wedding day?' he asked sheepishly.

'Of course it was,' she said. 'I know your memory is probably not as good as it once was, but don't you remember, we booked it for the last day in September? That was today, 30 September.'

'Yes, I remember,' he replied. 'It's just that I thought September had thirty-one days.'

## MISLEADING IMAGE

An elderly woman phoned the emergency services in Zurich, Switzerland, to report that her TV set was on fire. But when fire crews arrived at her home, they quickly ascertained that there was no blaze – it was simply that the television was tuned to a German channel that broadcasts a constant glowing-fireplace image in the early hours of the morning.

'The fire was extinguished with the press of a button,' commented a fire service spokesman.

---

**THE TRUTH HURTS**

Rose: Can I ask a dumb question?
Dorothy: Better than anybody I know.
THE GOLDEN GIRLS

---

## CHEWY CANDY

While watching TV one day at her Idaho home in 2009, eighty-seven-year-old Violet Bishop fancied a snack. She decided to dip into a box of chocolates that she had bought for Halloween trick-or-treaters. But one of them was so chewy she had to remove it from her mouth – and that's when she realized it was her hearing aid, which had fallen out of her ear and into the box.

'As I ate the Milk Duds,' she recalled later, 'I was aware that one was not as fresh as the others. It was rather crunchy and I just could not get it to soften up, no matter how hard I tried.'

## DISAPPEARING ACT

Jane's widowed father came to live with her but for months he struggled to find his way around the large family house. Every door looked the same to him and time after time he would mistake the closet for his bedroom and spend a few minutes in there before realizing that he was in the wrong room. No matter how often they told him, he had always forgotten by the following day, and soon Dad's wanderings became part of family life. But at least they knew that if they couldn't find him,chances were he would be in the closet.

One evening Jane and her husband threw a dinner party for a dozen friends. She invited her father because she thought he would enjoy the company but, although all the guests had arrived, he had done another of his disappearing acts. In despair she eventually asked her husband in a louder voice than she had intended, 'Isn't it time Dad came out of the closet?' The whole room fell silent.

## SAFETY IN NUMBERS

A little girl was sitting on her grandfather's lap when she asked him, 'Grandad, why do you need three pairs of glasses?'
'Well,' Grandad explained, 'I have one pair for long distance, another pair for reading – and the third pair to look for the other two.'

## FIRST TIME

After enjoying good health for seventy-six years, Arnold was admitted to hospital for the first time. Familiarizing himself with his new surroundings, he began playing with the bell cord which had been connected to his bed.

'What's this for?' he asked his son.

'It's a bell,' replied the son.

Arnold proceeded to pull it three times.

'I can't hear it ringing,' he said.

'No,' explained his son patiently, 'it doesn't ring. It switches on a light in the hall for the nurse.'

'Huh!' grumbled Arnold. 'I don't think much of that. If the nurse wants a light on in the hall, she can damn well switch it on herself!'

## DISTINCTIVE HAT

Sir Benjamin Collins Brodie, the eminent nineteenth-century British surgeon, was dedicated to his work and regarded social events as an unwelcome interruption. One evening, against his better judgement, he was persuaded to attend a fashionable party but, having shown his face for half an hour or so, decided to head to the men's room before making an early exit. He emerged wearing his hat and walked past a number of guests who were just arriving. He couldn't help noticing that they were sniggering at him, but he thought nothing more of it, attributing it to an excess of high spirits. Then, in the hall, he was accosted by the host.

'My dear Brodie,' he said, glancing at the surgeon's head, 'is that a normal part of your attire?'

When Brodie removed his headgear, he realized that, instead of collecting his hat from the men's room, he had absent-mindedly picked up the toilet seat cover.

## OUT OF GAS

We all have days when we're sure there's something we've forgotten to do but we can't remember for the life of us what it is. On that basis, perhaps we should sympathize with the two men who robbed a gas station in New York State but were caught because they forgot to fill up their getaway car with petrol while doing so. Police officers said they found the pair a mile away at the side of the road looking dejectedly at their car, which had run out of fuel.

## FORTY PLUS

'Life begins at forty – but so do fallen arches, rheumatism, faulty eyesight, and the tendency to tell a story to the same person three or four times.'
HELEN ROWLAND, JOURNALIST AND HUMORIST

## DINNER PARTY

Although a relatively minor poet himself, English clergyman the Reverend William Lisle Bowles counted among his friends such eminent poets as Samuel Taylor Coleridge and William Wordsworth. Perhaps one of the reasons why Bowles never scaled greater heights was because he had a memory like a sieve.

One evening, he invited his friends to a dinner party but failed to appear. Finally his wife went upstairs to see what was keeping him and found him searching all over his room for a stocking. After hunting high and low for the missing garment, Mrs Bowles discovered that her husband had put two stockings on one foot while his mind was preoccupied with his latest poem.

Bowles' daily journey to work took him through a turnpike gate at which he was required to pay two pence in order to allow his horse through. One day he passed through the gate on foot but still offered the gatekeeper the toll money.

'What's that for?' inquired the gatekeeper.

'For my horse, of course,' answered Bowles.

'But, sir, you have no horse today.'

'Oh,' said a surprised Bowles. 'Am I walking?'

## WHERE THERE'S A WILL …

An English firm of solicitors revealed in 2010 that the distribution of a man's will was delayed because he had suffered a senior moment while compiling it. When Leslie Fawdon drafted his will, he left half of his estate to his nephew, whom he named as 'Mark Parkinson'. Unfortunately he had no nephew of that name, but he *did* have a great-nephew named Justin Parkinson. Furthermore, no one by the name of Mark Parkinson had ever lived at the address mentioned in the will. A court eventually decided that Mr Fawdon had intended to benefit his great-nephew and awarded him a half-share in the estate.

## AN ALARMING EXPERIENCE

Being a heavy sleeper, Jo always set her alarm clock for six o'clock in the morning so that she wouldn't be late for work. She usually went to bed around midnight and found that six hours of sleep was all she needed. But one morning when her alarm went off, she still felt decidedly bleary-eyed. In fact, she felt so tired that she was tempted to stay in bed for another hour and tell her boss that her train had been cancelled. Ultimately, however, she was too conscientious to take that risk.

So she scrambled out of bed, her eyes half shut, and stumbled into the bathroom. Why did she feel so tired? Was it that extra glass of wine the previous evening? Or was she sickening for something? She had a shower, got dressed and went downstairs for breakfast, convinced by now that she must be going down with a bug. Curiously the morning paper wasn't lying in the porch and there was hardly any traffic outside. The world seemed eerily quiet. Perhaps, she thought, everyone was having a lie-in.

Still half-asleep despite her toast and tea, she brushed her teeth before going back to the bedroom to fetch her jacket for work. Out of the corner of her eye she noticed that her mobile phone on the dressing table was illuminated. It announced the time in large letters: 3.23. Aaaargh! It hadn't been her alarm clock going off at all – it was her phone provider sending her a message about a special offer on night-time calls.

As Jo came to terms with the horror of having got up three hours early, she made two important decisions: in future she would keep her phone switched off at night – and change her provider at the first opportunity.

## UNLUCKY DAY

While waiting for her boyfriend to grab the money from a US convenience store during a raid, a woman spotted a competition entry form on the counter. Thinking it might be her lucky day, she filled out the form, complete with her name, address and phone number. She realized it wasn't her lucky day when she was arrested a few hours later, having absent-mindedly left the form behind in the store.

## BEST SUPPORTING BACON SLICER

In his excellent book, *Great Showbiz and Theatrical Anecdotes*, Ned Sherrin recounts the story of a television casting director who, while drinking in a London club, spotted an actor and went over to congratulate him.

'You were very good at the National,' enthused the casting director.

'I'm sorry, I've never worked at the National,' replied the actor.

'I know I've seen you somewhere. Maybe it was the Royal Shakespeare Company?'

'I've never been with the RSC either.'

'I know I've seen you somewhere. Where have you been working?'

'To tell you the truth, I haven't had a job for years. I've been working on the bacon counter in the Food Hall at Harrods.'

'That's where I saw you! You were fantastic!'

## WARNING LABEL

When her father came to stay for Christmas, a young woman
noticed that he appeared to be avoiding his grandchildren.

'Is something the matter?' she asked. 'Usually you love
playing with them.'

'It's my new medication,' he explained, producing a bottle of
pills from his pocket. 'Here. Read the label.'

Taking the bottle, she read the label.

'Take three pills a day,' it said. 'KEEP AWAY FROM CHILDREN.'

### SANDWICH SURPRISE

One of the best things about losing your memory is
that you're always surprised to find out what's in
your sandwiches – if only you could remember
where you left your lunchbox.

## JUGGLING ACT

A juggler was driving to a show when he was stopped by a police
officer who became suspicious on finding matches and lighter fuel
in the glove compartment.

'What are these for?' asked the officer.

'I'm a circus juggler,' replied the driver. 'I need them for my act.'

The officer wasn't convinced and demanded proof. So the
driver picked up his props and began juggling three blazing

torches at the roadside, before taking things up a notch by closing his eyes and balancing on one leg.

Just then an elderly couple drove by. The husband turned to his wife and said, 'I'm so glad I quit drinking. Look at the test they have to do now!'

## ENGROSSED IN HER WORK

According to the husband of American novelist Anne Rivers Siddons, she becomes so distracted when about to start work on a new book that she once put the orange juice carton outside the back door and the kitten in the refrigerator.

## FATAL MISUNDERSTANDING

A woman visited the doctor's office to get some medication for her elderly husband. The doctor said, 'I want him to take two of these pills every Monday, Tuesday and Wednesday and then skip the remaining days of the week.'

Three weeks later, the woman returned to inform the doctor that her husband had died of a heart attack.

'I'm so sorry to hear that,' said the doctor. 'I just don't understand it. Your husband had no history of heart trouble. I hope it wasn't a side effect of the medication.'

'Oh, no,' said the wife. 'The pills were fine. It was the skipping that killed him.'

## BILL'S BOX

Former Microsoft CEO Bill Gates showed he has a sense of humour by acting out a senior moment in a 2008 leaving video that was shown to work colleagues. The video showed Gates exiting the office carrying his desk belongings in a box and then putting the box on the roof of his car while he opened the door. After starting the car, he drove away, completely forgetting about the box, which fell off the roof and scattered its contents on the ground.

> ### SHORT MEMORY
>
> A man collecting in a shopping mall asked a woman for a donation to an Alzheimer's charity.
> 'But I already gave to you just now,' she said. 'Don't you remember?'

## SMART EXIT

When influential German mathematician David Hilbert taught at Göttingen University in the early twentieth century, there was a tradition whereby each new faculty member, wearing black coat and top hat, would pay a short, formal visit to the various professors.

Hilbert was working at home one day when a young man thus attired knocked on his front door. Hilbert's wife showed him in and the young man, placing his top hat on the floor, entered into polite conversation with the professor. After a few minutes of idle chat, Hilbert, no doubt eager to get back to work, became impatient. Suddenly he leaped to his feet, picked up the visitor's top hat from the floor and placed it on his own head. Taking his wife by the arm, he said, 'My dear, I do think we have delayed our good colleague long enough,' and proceeded to march out of his own home.

## MILK MONITOR

Entering his examining room, a doctor found a woman and baby waiting for him. The doctor gave the baby a thorough check-up but was concerned that it wasn't gaining sufficient weight.

'Tell me,' he said to the mother, 'is the baby breast-fed or bottle-fed?'

'Breast-fed,' she replied.

'I see,' said the doctor.

He instructed the woman to strip down to her waist and then proceeded to knead and pinch both of her breasts. Motioning her to get dressed, he continued, 'It's clear what the problem is. No wonder this baby is hungry. You're not producing any milk.'

'I know,' said the woman. 'I'm his grandmother. But I'm really glad I came!'

## MAGIC ROUNDABOUT

We all know how daunting busy roundabouts can be, but one confused German driver had to be rescued by police after going round more than fifty times in her attempt to find an exit. Sixty-two-year-old Andrea Zimmer said of her adventure, 'I was breaking in a new car to see how it does in traffic and I couldn't seem to get to one of the exits. But I have to admit I got a very good feel for my new car and its handling. I think I can safely say it takes roundabouts pretty well.'

## SPORTING SENIOR MOMENTS

You'd expect sportsmen always to be on the ball, supremely focused in mind and body. But as these individuals prove, they can be just as susceptible to senior moments as the rest of us:

Making his way to the 1906 Olympics in Athens, Canadian pole-vaulter Ed Archibald somehow managed to lose his pole on the train journey through Italy.

Caddie Miles Byrne inadvertently put an extra club in Ian Woosnam's golf bag at the 2001 British Open, as a result of which Woosnam was given a two-stroke penalty that cost him £200,000 in prize money.

Plymouth Argyle football manager Paul Mariner was so overjoyed with his team's victory at Ipswich in 2010 that by way of celebration he threw his coat into the crowd … forgetting that his glasses were in the pocket.

After driving 3,000 miles across Europe in the 2000 Gumball Rally, Germany's Georg Etterer crashed his Mercedes just thirty metres from the finish line in Hampshire because he momentarily forgot that the English drive on the left.

Riding in a race at Wolverhampton in 1997, jockey Carl Lowther thought he had ridden the perfect finish on his horse Naval Games – only to realize as the rest of the field swept by that he had miscounted and there was still another circuit to go.

Easily leading the runners into the stadium near the end of the 1954 European Championships marathon in Berne, Russian athlete Ivan Filin turned the wrong way, lost over 100 metres and could finish only third.

After being not out overnight against Surrey at the Oval in 1921, Leicestershire cricketer Thomas Sidwell was unable to resume his innings the following morning because he got lost on the London Underground.

In 1936, Dr Tucker, a keen New Orleans golfer, put his name down for a hole-in-one tournament. Such was his enthusiasm that no sooner had he entered than he marched straight out to the competition hole to stake his claim – and was delighted to achieve a hole-in-one. Rushing back to the clubhouse to relay the good news, he was somewhat deflated to be informed that the competition didn't start for another two weeks.

## A NEW PHONE

Reasoning that it would help him keep in contact with her when she was out of the house, a son decided to buy his elderly mother a mobile phone for her birthday. Patiently he explained to her how the phone worked and went through all of its various features. She was delighted with it.

The next day, she was in town enjoying a morning break while shopping, when her phone rang. It was her son.

'Hello, Mum,' he said. 'How do you like your new phone?'

'I love it,' she replied. 'It's so compact, and your voice is really clear. And I love all the different features – the camera, the radio, the personal organizer and so on. It's wonderful. There's just one thing I don't understand, though.'

'What's that?' asked the son.

'How on earth did you know I was in Starbucks?'

---

### HIDE THE REMOTE

'George Bush sat at that desk in the White House with the button that could have ended the world. My father's younger than him and we don't give him the controls for the television.'

BILLY CONNOLLY, COMEDIAN

## LOST IN HIS WORK

It is never the most promising start to a marriage to forget your own wedding. Would Queen Victoria and Prince Albert have enjoyed such a happy marriage if he had absent-mindedly gone off for a game of golf on their wedding day? Would another of the world's great romantic couples, Marge and Homer Simpson, have stayed together for so long if she had been forced to drag him out of the donut shop on their big day?

Therefore it is a tribute to the tolerance of Marie Laurent that her union to eminent French chemist Louis Pasteur ultimately proved so enduring. Their wedding was fixed for 29 May 1849. All the guests arrived at the church but there was no sign of the groom. As concern mounted, a friend wondered whether Pasteur might still be in his laboratory, and sure enough that's where he found him, hard at work, oblivious to the fact that he was supposed to be getting married.

'Did you forget about your wedding?' asked the friend.

'Actually,' replied Pasteur, 'I did remember before I started this experiment but later I totally forgot. Thank God you came!'

## INCOMPLETE UNIFORM

Preparing to attend an important military engagement, Russian composer Alexander Borodin donned his finest plumed helmet and his army jacket laden with medals and walked out of the house glowing with an enormous sense of pride – until he realized that he hadn't put on the bottom half of his uniform …

## DISSATISFIED GUEST

An elderly lady from the country was visiting New York for the first time in her life. She checked in at a five-star hotel and watched as the porter took her bags. She followed him through the door, but then a look of intense disappointment came over her face.

'Young man,' she barked, 'I know I'm old and not used to the way you do things in the big city, but I'm not stupid. I paid a lot of money for this room and I was expecting a damn sight better than this. It's tiny, there's no window and no bathroom. Why, there's not even a bed!'

'Madam,' sighed the porter wearily, 'this isn't your room, It's the elevator.'

## REGAL ANECDOTES

King Charles II of England delighted in regaling his courtiers with stories about his colourful life, but these tales were not always appreciated by those who were hearing them for the umpteenth time. This led the Earl of Rochester to remark how surprising it was that someone who could remember every minute detail of a story could also fail to remember that he had related it to the very same people just the previous day.

## THAT'S HOW I KNOW YOU

English actor Walter Hudd enjoyed a forty-year career in which he graduated from provincial theatre tours to appearing in international movies. During one trip to the theatre as a member of the audience, he found himself sitting next to a man whose face seemed familiar. Throughout the first act, Hudd cast surreptitious glances in his neighbour's direction in the hope that the man's name would come to him. After half an hour of this, Hudd had become absolutely convinced that he knew the man, but simply could not remember where from.

At the interval, Hudd went to the bar and found the same man standing next to him. Unable to hold back any longer, Hudd said, 'Forgive me, but don't I know you?'

'Yes, you do,' replied the man. 'I'm your agent.'

## WIDOW TALK

Two elderly widows were talking about their late husbands. One asked the other, 'Did you have mutual orgasms?'
'No,' replied her friend, 'I think we were with the Prudential.'

## GOD ONLY KNOWS

Asked by members of the London Poetry Society for his interpretation of a particularly enigmatic passage in 'Sordello', Robert Browning shrugged his shoulders and replied, 'When I wrote that, God and I knew what it meant – but now God alone knows!'

## NEAR-DEATH EXPERIENCE

Thinking they had just sat through the cremation of their dear friend Roy Spencer, Gloucestershire pensioners Maurice and Shirley Dodwell were understandably surprised when they turned up to his wake and he answered the door. It transpired that they had been to the funeral of another Roy Spencer after spotting his name in the obituary column of the local newspaper.

## BLIND DATE

A man in his early sixties met a woman of a similar age on an internet chat room. They chatted every night for several weeks and got along so well that the woman eventually asked if they could meet in person.

'I'd really like that,' replied the man, 'but I have a confession to make. You see, I may have misled you slightly when describing myself. The truth is, I'm not exactly George Clooney. My whole face is covered in bright red boils, my nose is broken, I have a deep scar running across my forehead and I have a constant nervous twitch. I am four foot ten inches tall, chronically obese, completely bald, I have only one eye, and I've got a hunched back. But if you're still willing to meet me, I'll be waiting by the war memorial at one o'clock on Saturday.'

The woman wrote back: 'I am not at all worried about your appearance and am looking forward to meeting you on Saturday. But would you please carry a copy of *The Times* so that I can recognize you?'

## BE PREPARED

An old man decided to light a bonfire in his garden. He said to his wife, who was becoming increasingly forgetful, 'Did you bring the matches?'

'Yes, dear, I remembered,' she said, handing him the box.

So he set about starting the fire but, no matter how hard he tried, he couldn't get any of the matches to light.

'I don't understand,' said his wife. 'They should be fine. I tested them all before we came out.'

---

### AGE CONCERN

'In my local newspaper, they had this advert: "Please look after your neighbours in the cold weather." I live next door to this eighty-four-year-old woman, and do you know, not once has she come round to see if I'm all right. The lazy cow hasn't even taken her milk in for a fortnight.'

JACK DEE, COMEDIAN

---

## NO FIXED ABODE

In Mrs Claude Beddington's memoirs *All That I Have Met*, she recalled escorting the distinguished English stage actress Dame Ellen Terry to a charity matinee of *A Midsummer Night's Dream* at London's Drury Lane. This was during the First World War, by which time Dame Ellen was in her anecdotage and in possession of a memory that could best be described as transient. As they left the theatre and reached Mrs Beddington's car, Dame Ellen suddenly laughed, 'Isn't it funny, dearest? I can't remember where I'm living.'

Her companion recounted, 'She could only offer two clues: (1) that she was not staying in her own flat, and (2) that she must pass through something that looked like a churchyard with railings to reach the door.'

Fortunately, with a little help from the chauffeur, they were eventually able to deliver Dame Ellen to the right address.

## LATE STARTER

Near the end of her career, the formidable Argentine-born British actress Martita Hunt was rehearsing for a television play. As is the practice, at the end of each day's rehearsals, the production assistant handed out the call sheets for the following day.

'Miss Hunt,' said the PA, 'you're called at 9.45.'

'Quite impossible!' barked the actress.

'Why?'

'Because my bowels don't move until 10.15.'

## IMPAIRED VISION

Two veteran runners competing in a fifty-mile race around Rotherham, Yorkshire, made an unscheduled twenty-mile detour into Nottinghamshire because they forgot their glasses. Les Huxley, fifty-seven, and Barry Bedford, sixty-one, were unable to read the route map or see the race signposts, as a result of which they got hopelessly lost for eighteen hours. With the remaining 140 runners long finished and asleep in bed, the pair eventually crossed the line at 1.30am – but only after phoning the race organizer to come and fetch them.

## CENSUS TAKER

An old timer was sitting in his rocking chair on the porch of his Mississippi farmhouse when he was approached by a young man carrying a pen and clipboard.

'Whatever you're selling, son, I don't want it,' said the old man.

'I'm not selling anything. I'm the official census taker.'

'The what?! Well, you're not taking mine or they'll put me in a home for the confused.'

'No, no, you don't understand. We're simply trying to find out how many people there are in the United States.'

'Well, you're wasting your time with me,' shrugged the old man. 'I got no idea.'

## COLD COMFORT

A DJ on a radio station in Leicester thought he was way too young for a senior moment. He should be so lucky! One day, he lost his mobile phone. After searching the house for several hours, he finally gave up, accepting that he must have dropped it somewhere. Later that evening he heard it ringing and, tracing the sound to its point of origin, he duly found his mobile phone … in the fridge.

## CRIMINAL NEGLIGENCE

Some people really aren't suited to a life of crime. Take the two armed robbers who burst into a gas station in Rhode Island, sprayed a clerk in the face with pepper gas and snatched $157 from the cash register. Only then did they remember to put on ski masks, although one forgot to take the cigarette out of his mouth first and burned his face. The pair were easily identified on the store's security camera.

## MARRIAGE MYSTERY

In the *New York Times* of 25 October 1886, a correspondent recalled a telegram he had once received. It read, 'Under what name did I marry my wife two years ago? You were there, and hadn't as much to think about as I had. Please wire answer. Want to apply for divorce.'

## BRUCKNER IN THE BUFF

Advised by his doctor to take a daily bath, Austrian composer Anton Bruckner took to working in the tub on a regular basis. So preoccupied was he with composing in the bath that when the mother of a student knocked at the door of his apartment one day, he simply called out, 'Come in.'

She duly entered but was taken aback to find Bruckner in the bath. She was even more surprised when, dripping wet, he stepped out of the bath and walked over to greet her. It was only when she screamed and ran off that he realized he was naked.

## SIGNS OF AGEING

'First you forget names, then you forget faces, then you forget to zip up your fly, and then you forget to unzip your fly.'
BRANCH RICKEY, BASEBALL EXECUTIVE

## A GOOD EXCUSE

Ethel was driving along a Florida highway at speed when she was spotted by a Highway Patrol car. After chasing her for two miles, the officers finally managed to overtake her and force her to stop.

'Ma'am,' said one of the officers approaching her car ominously, 'do you know what speed you were doing?'

'Uh, no, officer, I'm afraid I don't,' replied Ethel softly.

'Well, I'll tell you. You were doing over 100, and unless you have a very good explanation for why you were driving that fast, I'm going to have to give you a speeding ticket.'

'Listen, officer,' said Ethel, 'I *do* have a reason for driving that fast. I'm eighty-one years old and my memory's not too good. So whenever I'm driving anywhere, I have to get there before I forget where I'm going.'

The officer scratched his head and waved her on her way.

## THE WRONG BERLIN

During the Second World War, Winston Churchill was greatly impressed by a series of dispatches he had received from the British Embassy in Washington. When he asked who had written them, he was told 'I. Berlin', referring to Isaiah Berlin, a member of the Embassy staff who would go on to become an outstanding philosopher.

In 1944, the songwriter Irving Berlin was in London to entertain the troops, and Mrs Churchill asked her husband whether it would be possible to thank him personally for his part in the war effort. It was then that Churchill experienced an unfortunate senior moment. Confusing the two I. Berlins, he insisted, to his wife's delight and surprise, that Irving Berlin should come to lunch.

It was a formal occasion, attended by a number of dignitaries, and at the head of the table Churchill questioned Berlin intently about American public opinion. To his dismay, he received only the vaguest of answers. When he pressed Berlin further and asked him what he thought was the most important thing that he had written, he was somewhat surprised to receive the reply: '"White Christmas"'.

At that point, according to observers, Churchill appeared to give up on the conversation.

### BEST FORGOTTEN

'Memories are like mulligatawny soup in a cheap restaurant. It is best not to stir them.'
– P.G. WODEHOUSE, AUTHOR

## HAVE WE MET BEFORE?

By the time British actress Margaret Halstan appeared in the West End production of *My Fair Lady* in the late 1950s, she was over eighty and rather frail. She was given the one-line role of the Queen of Carpathia, to whom Eliza Doolittle is introduced at the ball.

Each night after the show, the producer arranged for a taxi to take the veteran actress home. When it failed to arrive on one occasion, she was offered a lift by another member of the cast.

'And what part do you play, dear?' asked Halstan gently.

'I play Eliza Doolittle,' replied Julie Andrews.

## A HELPFUL MUGGER

It's comforting to know that criminals can be extremely co-operative – even if it's only because they've got the wrong end of the stick.

As a woman exited her local convenience store in New York, a thief snatched her purse. Luckily she was able to provide police officers with a detailed description of the mugger and a suspect was quickly apprehended. Officers then took him back to the store and told him to stand there for a positive ID. The suspect quietly did as he was told and when the victim appeared, he confirmed, 'Yes, officer, that's the woman I stole the purse from.'

## BIBLICAL CONNECTION

Sally had just started a new job and was naturally keen to make a good impression on her boss. So when he brought his six-year-old son into the office one morning, Sally desperately wanted to appear friendly to the boy.

'This is Joseph,' her boss announced. 'He'll be hanging out with me today.'

'Hi, Joseph,' beamed Sally, making a frantic mental note of his name because she had a terrible memory for people's names and what could be worse than getting the name of the boss's young son wrong on only your third day? Recalling a word-association tool she had read about, she said to herself, 'Joseph … Bible … Famous Biblical character … Just think "Bible".'

At the end of the day, her boss reappeared with the boy. Sally's mind immediately went blank and then she remembered the keyword 'Bible'.

'Bible, Bible, Bible,' she repeated silently before asking, 'And has young Herod enjoyed his day at the office?'

## FORGOTTEN FAMILY

Hollywood actress Drew Barrymore was asked in a magazine interview whether she hoped to have children one day.

'Definitely,' she replied. 'I would like to have at least two because I didn't have a brother or sister growing up … I mean, I have a brother but we didn't really spend a lot of time together … And I have a sister, too!'

## VISIBLE EMBARRASSMENT

One evening, American actress Julie Bowen and her TV colleagues visited an upmarket French restaurant in Greenwich, Connecticut. The restaurant's trademark feature was its bathrooms, which were fully see-through but had glass that frosted up when somebody walked in.

Julie was naturally curious to try them and eventually plucked up the courage, but shortly after sitting down she became aware that something wasn't quite right.

'I looked out and people were so *not* looking at me,' she recalled. 'I thought, "They're not looking because it's a two-way mirror." But then I thought, "People *always* look in mirrors ..." And I looked across the restaurant and I saw my boss at the table and I just knew from the way he glanced over and lowered his head ... You see, there was a button to activate the frost, but no one told me!'

## LOST IN THOUGHT

Albert Einstein was distracted even in his youth. Once he stayed overnight at a friend's house but when he left the following morning he forgot his suitcase. The friend's parents said to Einstein's parents, 'That young man will never amount to anything because he can't remember anything.'

During his spell at Princeton University in the 1930s, students loved to depict Einstein as an absent-minded professor. Albeit unintentionally, he did little to improve his reputation.

Someone once called the dean's office asking for directions.

'How do I get to Albert Einstein's home?' asked the caller.

When the man in the office said he couldn't give out that information, there was a pause on the other end of the line, followed by a long sigh and eventually the reply: 'This *is* Albert Einstein. I got lost walking home from the campus.'

## FLIGHT FRIGHT

After a particularly bumpy landing, the passengers were still shaking as they filed off the airplane. Even the crew were visibly pale as they uttered the standard farewell at the top of the steps.

Nevertheless none of the passengers mentioned the landing until the very last person off, a little old lady, gently inquired of one of the flight attendants, 'Tell me, dear, did we land or were we shot down?'

## FORGETTABLE FOOD

Mary Shelley, creator of *Frankenstein* and wife of romantic poet Percy Bysshe Shelley, regularly sent meals into her husband's study, but he frequently forgot to eat them. Later he would join her and ask, 'Mary, have I dined?'

Whether this was a comment on Shelley's absent-mindedness or on the quality of Mrs Shelley's cooking is not known.

## JUST LIKE MR BEAN

Addressing an awards ceremony, actor Rowan Atkinson – famous for his portrayal of the hapless Mr Bean – told the gathering, 'As I was leaving this morning, I said to myself, "The last thing you must do is forget your speech." And sure enough, as I left the house this morning, the last thing I did was to forget my speech.'

### CHANNEL HOPPING

'They always say that the older you get, you start to lose your memory. I could be watching a TV show for forty-five minutes, then during commercials, I start flipping through the channels. Then I have to stop and go, "What the hell was I watching?"'
JOHN HEFFRON, COMEDIAN

## ADVERTISING NIGHTMARES

Placing an advertisement in a newspaper or magazine should be a relatively straightforward exercise – unless, of course, you experience a senior moment and your words come out all wrong, as in the following that have appeared in publications around the world:

'One-week sale of blankets: These bargain lots are rapidly shrinking.'

'Man wanted to work in dynamite factory. Must be willing to travel.'

'Try our herbal remedies. You can't get better.'

'Wanted: Man to take care of cow that does not smoke or drink.'

'Ear piercing while you wait.'

'Mixing bowl designed to please a cook with round bottom for efficient beating.'

'Wasps' nests destroyed $40. OAPs $30.'

'School. Wanted in January. Experienced man to take almost entire responsibility for the lowest form of boys.'

'We will sell gasoline to anyone in a glass container.'

'Lost: Small apricot poodle – Reward. Neutered, like one of the family.'

'Sexual abuse centre looking for volunteers.'

'Used cars: Why go elsewhere to be cheated? Come here first.'

'Dog for sale. Eats anything, fond of children.'

'Man, honest. Will take anything.'

'Our bikinis are exciting. They are simply the tops!'

## BUS STOP

Finding herself in a strange city, a confused woman asked a police officer the way to the station.

'Wait here at this bus stop for bus number forty-two,' he said. 'It'll take you right there.'

Three hours later, the officer passed again and saw the woman still waiting at the bus stop.

'I said to wait for bus number forty-two,' he said. 'That was three hours ago. Why are you still waiting?'

'Don't worry,' said the woman. 'It shouldn't be long now. The thirty-ninth bus just went by.'

## TURNING A DEAF EAR

An elderly lady prided herself on being a careful driver. Whenever she took to the highway, she made sure she wore her seat belt, regularly checked her mirrors and always adhered to the speed limit. So on one of her weekly journeys to visit her sister, she was horrified to see in her rear-view mirror that a police patrol car was following her, lights flashing. She had no idea what she could have done wrong but being a law-abiding citizen she pulled over obediently.

The police patrolman walked up to her car window and started speaking but as he did so, the woman pointed to her ear and shook her head to indicate that she was deaf.

The patrolman smiled and signed back, 'I know. I'm here to tell you that your horn is stuck.'

## OLD ACQUAINTANCE

An acquaintance of actress Beatrice Lillie spotted her walking toward him down London's Piccadilly one day. The friend, who had not seen Miss Lillie for some years, manoeuvred himself into a position where she could not avoid bumping into him, and on doing so she immediately threw open her arms and embraced him warmly.

'Darling!' she gushed. 'How are you?'

Still holding him, she then leaned back and examined the friend's face before adding, 'And, more to the point, *who* are you?'

## MAILED TEETH

A grandmother was in such a hurry to mail her Christmas cards that she didn't notice that her new set of false teeth were wedged between them. Shortly afterward, she walked into the Post Office in Essex and announced to stunned staff and customers that she had accidentally posted her teeth in the collection box. Sensing stifled giggles, she said, 'It's no joke – I've had to put my old ones in!'

## CHANGE OF ADDRESS

After years of living in a small house, a university professor and his wife decided to move to a bigger home a quarter of a mile away. On the day of the move, the wife packed her absent-minded husband off to work with a note of their new address because she was sure that he would forget otherwise. He kept the note slightly protruding from the top pocket of his jacket to act as a constant reminder, but in the course of the busy day it fell out and, with nothing to jolt his memory, he automatically headed for his old address after work.

He arrived at his old house to find it all locked up. Then from somewhere in the dark recesses of his mind, he vaguely remembered something about moving house that day. But without the note, he had no idea of his new address.

Just then he spotted a young boy walking down the street.

'Excuse me, young man,' he said. 'I'm Professor Henderson, perhaps you know me. You see, we've just moved. I don't suppose you happen to know where we've moved to?'

'Sure, Dad,' said the boy. 'Come with me.'

---

### SILENCE IN COURT

'You never know how much a man can't remember until he is called as a witness.'
WILL ROGERS, HUMORIST

---

## MILITARY INTELLIGENCE

The mighty Prussian armies of the eighteenth century were spectacularly hindered on more than one occasion by the appalling eyesight of their officers, leading to a series of regrettable senior moments.

In 1757, the forces under Prince Augustus William were obliged to abandon the safest escape route when they saw the road ahead blocked by what they thought were batteries of Austrian artillery. The Austrian 'guns' turned out to be nothing more deadly than a herd of cattle. The same army panicked later on spotting what they took to be more guns. This time they burned all their own transport and pontoon bridges before realizing that the 'guns' were just tree trunks.

In the same year, another Prussian leader, Field Marshal Seydlitz, had managed to trap a French cavalry unit in a woodland hollow, only for one of his officers to fail to close the trap after mistaking young fir trees for advancing French infantrymen.

## MAHLER THE DREAMER

Austrian composer Gustav Mahler was something of a solitary dreamer. He was so absorbed in his work that he once studied a score for ages in a motionless train, unaware that the engine had been uncoupled. On other occasions he was known to absent-mindedly stir his tea with a lit cigarette.

Whenever he dined out, Mahler would rinse his glass before drinking from it but on a visit to a Budapest café with his sister Justi, he forgot himself, filled his glass with water and then emptied it over his shoulder, soaking a party of ladies on the terrace below. Although he immediately told the women how sorry he was for the lapse, his memory was so fragile that moments later he did the same thing with Justi's glass and had to apologize to them all over again.

## TOILET TIME

A senior lady consulted the doctor about her constipation.

'I haven't moved my bowels for ten days,' she said.

'Oh dear,' said the doctor. 'Yes, I can see why that would be a problem. Have you done anything about it?'

'Yes,' she replied. 'I sit in the toilet for three-quarters of an hour in the morning and then again in the evening.'

'No,' said the doctor. 'I mean do you take anything?'

'Of course I do,' she snapped. 'I take a book.'

## DIDN'T I MARRY HER?

While researching his 1985 biography of David Niven, author Sheridan Morley interviewed an ageing Lord Olivier about the 1939 movie version of *Wuthering Heights*, in which Merle Oberon had also starred. Above all, Morley wanted to know whether the rumour that Niven and Oberon had been lovers was true.

Olivier confirmed that it was indeed true but added, 'There's one thing you have to understand, that although Niven and I were both in love with Merle Oberon, I was the one who married her.'

'No, you didn't,' said Morley. 'You married Vivien Leigh.'

Olivier took in this information for a second before exclaiming, 'My dear boy, you are so right!'

## CAPTAIN'S LOG

Each time his ship took to sea, an elderly captain was seen to go to the safe, unlock it, take out a small red book, study it for a moment and then put it back in the safe. The other officers were curious about the contents of the mystery book but could never get hold of the old man's keys.

One day the captain died and, in accordance with tradition, was buried at sea. As soon as the ceremony was finished the first officer grabbed the keys and eagerly opened the safe. His hands trembling with anticipation, he took out the small red book, opened it and saw that it contained a single entry: 'Port is on the left; starboard on the right.'

## MULTI-TASKING

Two elderly gents were chatting in their retirement home.

'I may be getting old,' said one, 'but at least I can multi-task now.'

'In what way?' asked the other.

'Well, these days, whenever I sneeze I pass gas.'

## A TALE OF TWO ROBSONS

When the late Bobby Robson was manager of the England football team in the 1980s, his trusted captain was Manchester United's Bryan Robson. Bobby would sometimes get confused with players' names and, while addressing his captain, once called him 'Bobby'. To which Bryan Robson helpfully pointed out, 'No, boss. I'm Bryan, you're Bobby.'

## THE NAME GAME

Zsa Zsa Gabor was once asked about her memory for names. She laughed, 'I don't remember anybody's name. How do you think the "daahling" thing got started?'

## FITNESS CLUB

A man in his sixties was chatting to his friend about the fitness club he had recently joined.

'I took part in an aerobics class for seniors,' he said.

'How did it go?' inquired the friend.

'Well, I bent, I twisted, I turned, I jumped up and down, and I sweated for an hour – but by the time I'd finally got my leotard on, the class had ended.'

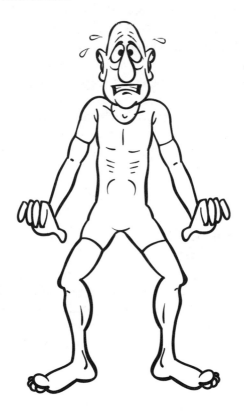

## BRUT FORCE AND IGNORANCE

It was a glittering showbiz award ceremony, the sort where the great and the good of the television industry pat themselves on the back for three hours. A sumptuous six-course meal was laid on for the hundreds of black-tie guests, all of whom were given bags of designer goodies to take home afterwards. As an added touch, small bottles of ladies' perfume and men's aftershave were placed on the tables.

Among the guests was Harold, a senior TV executive who was nearing retirement age and whose concentration was inclined to waver occasionally. The first course was smoked mackerel, and a small green bottle of lemon juice sat on the table to be used as a dressing. Harold was so busy chatting to his fellow diners that he didn't pay sufficient attention to which bottle he was picking up and, before he knew it, he had soaked his mackerel with the great smell of Brut. He only needed one mouthful to realize his mistake and to discover why fish tend not to wear aftershave.

## QUICK RETURN

A patient on his way out of hospital ended up back inside after his elderly mother ran him over when she came to collect him in her car. Ron Carter had just been discharged from Elliot Hospital, New Hampshire, and was walking to meet his eighty-four-year-old mother Lillian when she accidentally hit him.

## LATE CALLER

Eighteenth-century German writer and philosopher Gotthold Lessing was renowned for his fragile memory. Arriving home late one evening and realizing that he had forgotten his key, he knocked on the front door. A servant appeared at a window but, unable to recognize his master in the dark, called out, 'The professor isn't home.'

'Very well,' Lessing replied, walking off. 'Tell him I'll call another time.'

---

### CHANGING TIMES

'In youth we run into difficulties; in old age difficulties run into us.'
BEVERLY SILLS, SOPRANO

---

## SELECTIVE MEMORY

In the course of a shoot, the esteemed New York portrait photographer Jill Krementz asked author Janet Flanner whether she had ever been married.

'I'm sure I have,' Flanner replied nonchalantly, 'but the precise details of the union quite escape me.'

## I THOUGHT YOU HAD IT ...

To be fair, when you set off on a polar expedition there are a lot of things to remember – compass, thermals, seal recipe book. In 2002, Eric Phillips and Jon Muir became the first Australians to walk unaided to the North Pole, trekking across barren wastes for nearly two months, surviving frostbite, polar bears, and a near

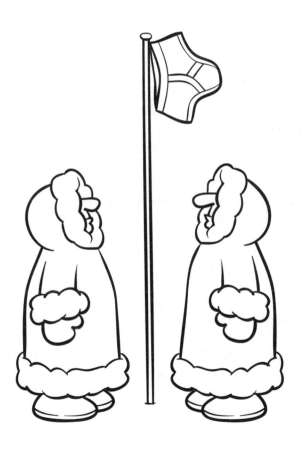

fatality after Muir fell through thin ice. Yet when they finally reached their destination, it suddenly dawned on them that they had nothing to mark their heroic deeds because they had forgotten to bring an Australian flag to plant at the Pole. If only they'd made a list ...

## TROLLEY DOLLY

On a transatlantic flight, an elderly man found himself sitting next to a Baptist minister. Since the flight had been delayed at take-off, the crew announced that, by way of an apology, all passengers would receive complimentary drinks.

When the pretty young flight attendant came round with the drinks trolley, the old man asked her for a gin and tonic. She then asked the Baptist minister what he would like to drink.

'I would rather commit adultery than drink alcohol!' he raged.

'I'm terribly sorry,' said the old man, handing his drink back to the attendant, 'I didn't realize there was a choice.'

## OUT TO LUNCH

The proprietor of a small country store had the memory span of a goldfish. One day he went out to lunch and came back to find a sign on the door saying 'Out to Lunch', so he sat down on the step to wait for himself.

## A SCREW LOOSE?

G.K. Chesterton, author of the *Father Brown* stories, lived in such a permanent daze that he rarely seemed in control of his actions. One day he approached the ticket window of a London train station and asked the clerk for a cup of coffee. When his error was pointed out to him, Chesterton apologized profusely, cleared his mind, marched into the station café and ordered a ticket to Battersea.

On another occasion, Chesterton required a corkscrew and went to the house next door to borrow one. Returning home, he was dismayed to find that he couldn't get back into his house – the key refused to work. It was then that he realized he was holding the key in his left hand and had been trying to unlock the door with the corkscrew.

## PAST HIS SELL-BY DATE

An elderly man was dozing in his chair one afternoon when he was awoken by a knock at the door. He slowly shuffled to the door and opened it to find a gorgeous young woman standing there.

'Oh, I'm sorry,' she smiled. 'I'm at the wrong house.'

'Sweetheart, you're at the right house,' the old man assured her, 'but you're thirty-five years too late!'

## RARE CONDITION

'I'm a psychic amnesiac. I know in advance what I'll forget.'
MIKE MCSHANE, COMEDIAN

## BABY TALK

Wendy was extremely proud of her first baby, so when her mother came to stay she suggested that she might like to see the baby have its bath. Afterwards Wendy asked her mother what she thought of the baby.

'Oh, it's a lovely baby,' said the mother, 'but tell me: is it a boy or a girl?'

'Have you lost your glasses?' laughed Wendy.

'No, dear,' replied the mother, 'but I *have* lost my memory.'

## TRAPPED IN A PHONE BOOTH

Billy Connolly once called his manager late at night with an urgent problem: he was standing in a phone booth and couldn't get out. His manager dutifully came to the rescue, by which time Connolly, still trapped inside, had fallen asleep. The comedian subsequently confirmed that the fault was entirely his own.

'There was nothing wrong with the booth – I just couldn't figure out which wall was the door!'

## WHAT A DRAG!

In the 2002 movie *Sorority Boys*, American actor Michael Rosenbaum (by then a youthful thirty) played one of three college boys who, having been wrongfully accused of embezzlement, decided to dress as girls in an effort to gain the evidence needed to prove their innocence.

On set one day, he was talking to a pretty girl but was aware that she didn't seem to be taking him seriously. Eventually he worked out what the problem was – he had forgotten that he was still in drag.

## WHEN IN DOUBT, WRITE A LIST

A sure sign of senior-momentitis is the inability to perform any multiple task without first writing a list. We can no longer rely on our memory alone, whether we are buying a few items from the grocery store, getting Christmas presents or even putting on socks in the morning. We have to make a list: 1. Right sock 2. Left sock.

How two men who carried out a burglary in Tallahassee, Florida, must have wished that they had made a list before they set out! They were arrested after unwisely going back to the house from which they had stolen two TV sets, only to find that the police had already arrived.

And the reason the burglars went back? They had forgotten to steal the remotes for the TVs.

## FLAWED GETAWAY

There is never a good time to lock your car keys inside your car – but probably the worst time to choose is when you have just robbed a bank and are looking to make a quick getaway. A Virginia robber had already dropped a trail of $100 bills in his wake as he fled the bank, but then found to his horror that he had no access to his getaway car. To reach the elusive keys, he smashed the car window with a large piece of wood, an action that alerted passers-by and led to his swift arrest.

## IN LOVING MEMORY

Towards the end of his life, nineteenth-century American poet Ralph Waldo Emerson had terrible trouble with his memory. He used to forget his own name sometimes, as well as the names of everyday objects, which he would instead describe in a roundabout manner. For example, if he saw a plough he would call it 'the implement that cultivates the soil'.

Emerson became increasingly embarrassed about his forgetfulness and started to restrict his public appearances. He did make an exception to attend the funeral of Henry Wadsworth Longfellow, but partway through the ceremony he turned to a fellow mourner and sighed, 'The gentleman has a sweet, beautiful soul – but I have entirely forgotten his name!'

## NEW NEIGHBOURHOOD

Writing in North Carolina's *Salisbury Post* newspaper, columnist Jennifer Doering described a senior moment she experienced a week after her wedding. She and her husband had driven from Wisconsin to their new home near Sacramento, California. With no furnishings, electricity or water, they spent the first night sleeping on the floor. Early the next morning, Jennifer decided to drive to the nearest store to pick up urgently needed cleaning supplies and food, while her husband stayed behind at the house waiting for the electric and telephone people to arrive.

She left their driveway, passing a big school bus that was parked at the roadside, and headed into town. After completing her errands, she set off on the return journey, following the rough map her husband had drawn for her. Alas, she got hopelessly lost and ended up driving around in circles for an hour. By the time she drove down an unmarked road and stopped at someone's house to ask for directions, she was feeling apprehensive and quite bewildered. She was beginning to wonder if she would ever see her new home and husband again.

When a lady answered the door, Jennifer asked, 'Do you know where 1880-D Vierra Lane is?'

The woman looked at her incredulously and replied, 'Oh, you must be the newlywed – you live right next door! Welcome to our neighbourhood!'

Jennifer's brain had not only failed to absorb the big school bus that was still parked outside, but she had also failed to spot her husband standing at the end of the driveway, waving frantically and wondering why she had driven right past him.

## TOO MANY HANDS

An absent-minded man arrived home from work to find that someone had stolen his wallet.

'How did that happen?' demanded his wife. 'How come you didn't feel a hand in your pocket?'

'I did,' replied the man, 'but I thought it was mine.'

## FIGHT THE GREY

'There is only one cure for grey hair. It was invented by a Frenchman. It's called the guillotine.'
– P.G. WODEHOUSE, AUTHOR

## SENIOR LOGIC

Two elderly men were sitting on a park bench watching the world go by when one suddenly turned to the other and said, 'I wish I knew where I was going to die.'

'Why do you want to know that?' asked his friend.

'Isn't it obvious? So that I can avoid ever going there!'

## OWN GOAL

Jock Coll, the trainer of the United States soccer team, had a very public senior moment at the 1930 World Cup. During the semi-final, opponents Argentina scored a hotly-disputed goal and Coll was still fuming about this when he was called upon to run onto the pitch and treat an injured American player. Still seething with rage, he pointedly threw down his medical bag, breaking a bottle of chloroform in the process and accidentally anaesthetizing himself. He consequently suffered the indignation of being carried off the pitch by his own team.

## HIS NUMBER'S UP

A woman was accompanying her husband on a business trip abroad. He was carrying his laptop computer with him, and the security officer at the airport asked him to open the case. It was locked, and the officer had to wait patiently while the husband tried to remember the combination. After about ten minutes, by which time his hands and head were drenched in sweat, the husband finally remembered the combination and opened the case.

Afterwards his wife asked him, 'Why were you so nervous?'

He confessed sheepishly, 'Because the numbers are the date of our wedding anniversary.'

## CONFUSING COWS

None of us likes to admit that our eyesight is not as good as it used to be. But American novelist Tom Wolfe – author of *The Bonfire of the Vanities* – probably booked a trip to the optician as soon as he returned from a skiing vacation in New England.

He recalled, 'We were in New Hampshire or Vermont, and we drove by a field of Holstein cows. I was trying to show what a country man I am, and so I said, "You'll notice that all those cattle are facing in the same direction – that's very typical."'

Rarely has the saying 'pride comes before a fall' been more appropriate – for on closer inspection, it emerged that the cows were all stuffed toys, and only about half the size of regular cows.

## TARGET PRACTICE

Two men were enjoying a seaside lunch in the sunshine when a seagull that was flying overhead pooped on the bald head of one of the men.

'Don't worry,' said a nearby waitress, 'I'll run and fetch some toilet paper.'

As she hurried off, one of the men turned to the other and said, 'How crazy is she! That bird'll be miles away by the time she gets back!'

## THE BIG HAND IS ON ...

American sprinters Eddie Hart and Rey Robinson, who were among the favourites for the men's 100 metres at the 1972 Munich Olympics, were disqualified from the event after failing to appear for their second-round heats because their coach had a senior moment while reading the starting time. The coach had told them the race would be run in the evening, but it was in fact being staged in the afternoon. Waiting for the team bus a few miles away at the Olympic village, Robinson was watching television when he suddenly realized that the athletes on screen were lining up for the race in which he was supposed to be running!

## WHERE ARE WE?

When former British Prime Minister Sir Alec Douglas-Home was appointed Foreign Secretary by Edward Heath in 1970, he was already in his late sixties. Understandably he found the succession of state visits exhausting and not a little confusing. It is said that whenever he landed in a foreign country, his devoted wife Elizabeth would constantly repeat the name of the city to him as she walked behind him down the steps of the aeroplane: 'Peking, Alec. Peking, Peking.' This was to prevent him declaring to his hosts in front of the world's press how delighted he was to be back in Montreal.

## THE TRIALS OF GRANDCHILDREN

'Grandchildren can be annoying. How many times can you go, "And the cow goes moo and the pig goes oink"? It's like talking to a supermodel.'
JOAN RIVERS, COMEDIENNE

## GLYNIS WHO?

In his later years, Sir Rex Harrison had difficulty remembering lines – and sometimes names. His last stage appearance was in *The Circle* with Glynis Johns and Stewart Granger. During the pre-Broadway tour of the show, Harrison was asked by a visiting English producer, 'How is Glynis?'

'Glynis who?' queried Harrison.

'Glynis Johns.'

'No idea. Lovely girl. Haven't seen her for years.'

## WRONG ROUTE

Two old ladies were waiting at a bus stop. A bus pulled up, and one of the old ladies asked the driver, 'Will this bus take me to the train station?'

'No, sorry,' said the driver.

The other old lady asked, 'Will it take me?'

## HIGHWAY PERIL

An elderly man was driving along the highway when his mobile phone rang. It was his wife.

'Stanley,' she said with some urgency, 'I've just heard on the news that there's a car travelling the wrong way on the highway. So please be careful.'

'*One* car?' screamed Stanley. 'There are hundreds of them!'

## TIRING JOURNEY

After a twenty-five-minute bus journey, Betty arrived at her daughter's house looking tired and agitated.

'Are you all right, Mother?' asked her daughter.

'Not really, dear,' said Betty. 'I feel a little nauseous from sitting backwards on the bus.'

'Oh, you poor thing. Why didn't you ask the person opposite you to swap seats?'

'I couldn't,' said Betty. 'That seat was empty.'

## FRIENDLY WARNING

German physicist Max Planck was just thirty-four when, in 1892, he was made a full professor at the University of Berlin. One day, while he was still settling in there, he forgot which room he had been assigned for a lecture and called in to the university office to find out.

'Could you tell me,' he asked the elderly man in charge of the office, 'in which room Professor Planck is lecturing today?'

The old man gave him a friendly pat on the shoulder.

'Don't go there,' he advised. 'You are much too young to understand the lectures of our learned Professor Planck!'

## WANDERING MIND

Rose: This is like *The Long Day's Journey Into Light*.
Dorothy [correcting her]: *Night*, Rose.
Rose [heading to her room]: Night, Dorothy.
THE GOLDEN GIRLS

## THE NAME ESCAPES ME

Singer Rod Stewart revealed that his 1971 hit 'Maggie May' had
been inspired by 'one of the first if not the first woman I ever
loved'. He went on to explain that 'Maggie May' was not her real
name but had been used for lyrical reasons because he couldn't
actually remember her real name.

## WHERE AM I?

On a hectic book tour of the United States, American writer
Studs Terkel checked into so many motels in different towns and
cities that he started to lose track of place and time.

At one motel, he asked the operator, 'Could you please wake
me up at six o'clock because I've got to get the eight o'clock
plane to Cleveland.'

There was a pause on the other end of the line before the
operator replied, 'Sir, you *are* in Cleveland.'

## NO ENTRY

A woman arrived for her stay at a smart modern hotel. The desk clerk handed her the room card, and directed her to her room. There, she took the card from her handbag but simply couldn't get the door to open. In despair, she eventually returned to reception.

'This room card doesn't work,' she complained. 'I've tried and tried and tried but the door won't open. This modern technology's a total waste of time. What's wrong with good old keys? You never had problems with keys. Damn stupid cards!'

With that she handed the card to the clerk.

'What you say may well be true, madam,' he said, turning the card over in his hands, 'but I suspect that the real reason you have been unable to gain access to your room is because you've been trying to open the door with your library card ...'

## DOUBLE TROUBLE

A New Zealand woman suffered a spectacular attack of senior-momentitis in 2010 when she managed to run over her husband – twice. As she reversed the family's four-wheel-drive vehicle down the driveway, she accidentally ran over her sixty-nine-year-old husband. Unaware of what had happened, she then drove forward and ran him over again. While he was treated in hospital for moderate head, chest and back injuries, his wife was said to be 'distraught'.

## DIDN'T WE BRING MUM?

Many a man has tried to forget his mother-in-law, but a husband from Merseyside took it to extremes in 2010 by accidentally abandoning his wife's mother in a multi-storey car park for over six hours. The man and his wife drove 300 miles from their home to Dover with the intention of taking her mother on a day trip to France. But after parking their vehicle in a long-stay car park, they forgot all about the old lady on the back seat and boarded the cross-channel ferry. It was only when they docked in France that the absent-minded pair remembered that Mum was still back in England. They caught the next ferry back to Dover ... where she was waiting to give them hell.

## EDISON'S LAPSE

Thomas Edison may have been responsible for more than a thousand inventions but that didn't stop him having the occasional senior moment. Having gone to the local court house to pay his taxes, Edison was asked for his name by the clerk. For some ironic reason, the light bulb in his head failed to illuminate his brain, leaving Edison unable to come up with an answer and staring blankly at the other people in the queue. Thus nobody present knew that the man who couldn't remember his own name was actually one of America's greatest ever scientists.

## THE NAKED TRUTH

One morning, June saw her husband off to work as usual before going upstairs to run a bath. As she put her foot in the water, she suddenly remembered that she had forgotten to switch off the gas cooker after breakfast. *Ha, another senior moment*, she thought. Since there was nobody else in the house, she didn't bother putting on her bathrobe before going downstairs to turn off the gas. Walking into the kitchen, she switched off the gas but as she did so, she heard footsteps approaching the back door.

She had an arrangement with the milkman whereby he brought the milk bottles into the kitchen to prevent the birds from drinking the cream. Not wanting to be caught naked, she made a dash for the broom cupboard and shut the door behind her.

From her hiding place, she heard the back door open and the footsteps come into the kitchen. But then, to her horror, they continued across the kitchen and suddenly the broom cupboard door was flung wide open. It was the gas man, who had come to read the meter next to which June was standing.

Staring back at him stark naked, June struggled to think of a plausible explanation. Eventually she said meekly, 'I'm sorry, I was expecting the milkman.'

## MEMORIES, MEMORIES

Alec and Ted were sitting at the window table of a café when a pretty young girl walked quickly along the street outside hotly pursued by a young man.

'Did you see that?' asked Alec. 'That young man chasing that pretty girl? Do you remember how you and I used to chase pretty girls?'

'Ah, yes, I remember *how* we used to chase them,' sighed Ted, 'but I can't for the life of me remember *why.*'

## CAROL'S CLANGER

After recording an episode of the TV word game *Countdown*, Carol Vorderman was chatting to broadcaster, author and producer Ned Sherrin, who was a guest on that day's show. She mentioned the stage production *Ziegfeld*, which had recently opened in London's West End to hugely disappointing reviews, and asked Sherrin whether he had seen it.

'Yes, darling,' he replied. 'I wrote it.'

---

### AGE BENEFIT

'The greatest part about getting really old: your memory starts going. That's a treat. It makes marriage go a lot easier. You come down in the morning: "Oh, who's this young lady cooking me eggs?"'

TOM PAPA, COMEDIAN

## EXTRA COAT

On a warm summer's day, a woman was surprised to see her neighbour painting his garden shed while wearing a raincoat over a thick woollen jacket.

'Aren't you hot?' she called out.

'Yes, I am a bit,' he replied breathlessly.

'Then why are you wearing all those clothes on a day like this?'

'Because,' he answered, 'it says here on the tin: "For best results, put on two coats."'

## ABANDONED BY 'THE DUKE'

The older we get, the more our minds tend to play tricks on us. Shoes get up and walk from one room to another, keys hide themselves in pockets we never use, and next-door neighbours change their names without telling us. Actress Dame Thora Hird was ninety-one by the time she died in 2003, so she was entitled to the odd day when she wasn't perhaps at her sharpest.

On one occasion near the end of her life, Dame Thora phoned her daughter, Janette Scott, to say that she was filming with John Wayne and that he had left her alone on the set.

Janette thought it unlikely, largely because John Wayne had died in 1979 and also because she was certain her mother was at home.

'Look out of the window, Mum,' she urged. 'Can't you see the mews?'

'Yes,' replied Dame Thora, still not convinced, 'but they can do wonderful things with scenery these days.'

## WALLPAPERING THE BEDROOM

One day, Maurice decided to redecorate the bedroom of his apartment. He wasn't sure how many rolls of wallpaper he would need but he knew his friend Sidney from next door had recently wallpapered his bedroom and the two rooms were identical in size.

'Sidney,' he asked, 'how many rolls of wallpaper did you buy for your bedroom?'

'Let me see now,' said Sidney. 'My memory's not what it used to be, but I've got the receipt somewhere.'

He shuffled off to look for the receipt and returned with the information: 'It was eight. I bought eight rolls.'

So Maurice bought eight rolls of wallpaper and eventually completed the job, but at the end he had two rolls left over.

The next time he saw Sidney he said, 'I bought eight rolls of wallpaper like you said, but I had two left over.'

'Yes,' said Sidney. 'So did I.'

## SHORT-SIGHTED

An English burglar must have wished he had taken his distance glasses with him before breaking into a shop in Bristol. For as a police officer on routine patrol duty passed the shop, which was closed for business, he was surprised to see someone waving to him from inside and immediately went to investigate. When arrested, the hapless burglar admitted that he had mistaken the officer for his accomplice.

## WHAT THE BUTLER SAW

On moving to Hollywood at the age of sixty-three to play the archetypal crusty Englishman in films such as *The Prisoner of Zenda*, C. Aubrey-Smith also took with him his love of cricket. He founded the Hollywood Cricket Club and recruited the likes of Errol Flynn, Boris Karloff and David Niven to its ranks.

His status in Hollywood (he was made Sir Charles Aubrey-Smith in 1944) meant that he could pretty much dictate the rules of the game. In one encounter, he was fielding close to the wicket when he dropped a catch. He immediately stopped the match and demanded that his butler be brought to the wicket. When the butler dutifully appeared, Sir Charles bellowed, 'Fetch me my glasses.'

Several minutes later, with play still suspended, the butler returned carrying the spectacles on a silver tray. They failed to have the desired effect and shortly afterwards Sir Charles dropped another catch. This prompted him to shout at his butler, 'Damn fool, you brought me my reading glasses!'

## COMEDY ROUTINE

A woman travelling on a train noticed that the elderly man sitting opposite her was behaving in a most unusual manner. He kept mumbling to himself, smiling, and then raising his hand. After he had repeated this routine a few times, she finally decided to ask him what he was doing.

He answered, 'These long rail journeys can get very boring,

so I pass the time by telling myself jokes.'

'Oh, I see,' said the woman. 'Well, that explains the mumbling and the smiling, but why do you also raise your hand?'

'Ah,' said the old man, 'that's to interrupt myself because I've heard that one before.'

## COMPARING NOTES

Three old men were bemoaning the effects of ageing. The first, a sixty-year-old, complained, 'I love music but my hearing isn't what it used to be and that means I can no longer appreciate the sounds. Deafness, my friends, is a terrible thing.'

The second, a seventy-year-old, moaned, 'I love art but my eyesight is now so bad that I can't see the delicate shades of the great masters. Loss of sight, my friends, is far worse.'

'My poor young friends,' sighed the third man, a nonagenarian. 'You have not begun to understand the true perils of old age. Yesterday I awoke next to my twenty-one-year-old mistress. The sunlight was playing on her bosom and I was filled with desire, so I said to her, "Darling, I wish to make love."

'"You old fool," she replied. "We made love only ten minutes ago!"

'You see, my friends, losing your memory is the most frightening failing of all.'

## SOMETHING MISSING

On his way home from a shopping trip, notoriously absent-minded scientist Sir Isaac Newton dismounted his horse so that it could have a rest, and then walked along leading the animal by its bridle. He became so distracted that it was only when he arrived home several hours later that he realized the horse had slipped its bridle long ago, and that he had completed the last few miles alone.

## FORGOTTEN INVITATION

We can get so preoccupied with what we are doing that we become oblivious to everything going on around us. How many of us have been so intent on grilling our bacon to perfection that we have failed to spot flames leaping from the toaster a few yards away? And what about the DIY enthusiast who is concentrating so hard on painting the most inaccessible corner of the ceiling that he doesn't realize his left foot is standing in a tray of white emulsion?

French physicist André Marie Ampère was someone who always threw himself wholeheartedly into his work – to the extent that, between the afternoon and evening of one day, he managed to forget completely a dinner invitation delivered personally by none other than the Emperor Napoleon.

On another memorable occasion, Ampère was so engrossed with the development of a new theory that he somehow managed to mistake the side of a horse-drawn delivery van for a blackboard. He began some hasty calculation on it before first walking and then running alongside it to continue his work as it drove off.

### TWO-MINUTE TEST

'When I meet a man whose name I can't remember, I give myself two minutes. Then, if it is a hopeless case, I always say, "And how is the old complaint?"'
BENJAMIN DISRAELI, POLITICIAN

## UNDER THE TABLE

At a seniors' lunch, a gentleman was delighted to find himself sitting next to the retirement home matron, a striking blonde in her late forties. During the course of the meal, he felt her leg pressing against his. At first he thought it was probably an accident but as the lunch progressed, he could still feel her leg pressing firmly against his. He could hardly believe his luck: an eighty-seven-year-old man being lusted after by matron!

He began to play 'footsie' under the table and, to his unbridled joy, her leg did not flinch in the slightest. He gave her knowing glances but she was playing it cool, the epitome of class. Finally he decided to take the plunge and slid his hand beneath the table to fondle her leg. That was when he discovered that his leg was pressed not against matron's, but against the table leg.

## WHAT AM I?

On her first visit to the United States, a senior lady was struck by the ingenious names given to public toilets. Instead of the plain old 'ladies' and 'gentlemen' that she was used to in England, she was confronted with 'guys' and 'dolls' or 'dudes' and 'dames'.

She coped without too much difficulty until visiting a small town in Wyoming. Needing to use the toilet in a hotel, she pondered the signs for ages before finally seeking help.

'Excuse me, bartender,' she asked politely, 'am I a heifer or a steer?'

## FOOD FOR THOUGHT

At a particular point in his afternoon lecture to students, an elderly professor of anatomy would ask the laboratory assistant to uncover a plastic box containing a specimen of a dead toad, beautifully dissected and displayed. One day, however, when the box cover was removed, instead of the toad there were two hardboiled eggs and a cheese sandwich.

'That's odd,' mused the professor, 'and I'm sure I ate my lunch ...'

## JUST TOO LATE

An American couple were among a coach party of seniors touring England. One lunchtime, their tour took them to Runnymede, where they saw a plaque that said, 'Magna Carta signed here 1215.'

The wife looked at her watch and then turned to her husband and said, 'Gee, Norm, what a shame! I guess we just missed it.'

## SHARP REMINDER

There are times when you can get away with having a senior moment without anybody knowing; when you are holding a three-foot-long sword in your hand is not one of those times. That is how an Indiana woman came to stab herself in the foot in 2008 while performing a religious ritual at a cemetery.

The Wiccan ceremony involves the driving of swords into the ground during a full moon, but the woman inadvertently put the sword into her left foot instead. Ironically she had performed the ritual to give thanks for a recent run of good luck.

## MIDNIGHT CALL

An elderly lady was woken by her phone ringing shortly after midnight. When she picked it up, the voice on the other end said, 'Is that the Arcadia Club?'

'No, dear, it's not,' said the old lady. 'This is a private residence.'

'I must have the wrong number. Sorry to trouble you at this time of night.'

'Oh, it's no trouble,' said the old lady. 'I had to get up anyway to answer the phone.'

### TOO MANY TO REMEMBER

During one of her later weddings (there have been eight weddings to seven husbands) Elizabeth Taylor was asked by an official to list her previous spouses.

'What is this,' Taylor replied, 'a memory test?'

## SIMPLE SOLUTION

Two senior ladies were discussing their husbands. One said, 'I do wish Maurice would stop biting his nails. It's such a nasty habit.'

Her friend said, 'My Wilfred used to do the same thing, but, you know, I eventually managed to cure him of the habit.'

'How did you do that?'

'Easy. I hid his teeth.'

## A LOSING BATTLE

An elderly lady went to see an attorney about a divorce.

'What grounds do you have, madam?' he asked.

'About six acres.'

'No, I don't think you quite understand. I'll put it another way. Do you have a grudge?'

'No, just a parking space.'

'I'll try again. Does your husband beat you?'

'No, I always get up at least an hour before he does.'

The attorney could see he was fighting a losing battle.

'Madam,' he sighed, 'are you sure you want a divorce?'

'I'm not the one who wants a divorce,' she said. 'My husband does. He claims we don't communicate.'

## FLAT HAT

On a visit to a Leipzig church to hear a rehearsal of one of his works, Hungarian composer Franz Liszt was dismayed to note that his precious silk hat had disappeared. His entourage searched the church high and low, but to no avail. Resigned to his loss, Liszt finally rose from his seat – and was embarrassed to discover that all he had in fact been sitting on his hat, which was now flattened beyond recognition.

## DENTIST DASH

Dame Judi Dench was filming the BBC period costume drama *Cranford* in 2009 when she broke off part of a tooth. With no time to waste, she was rushed, still in full costume, to the nearest dentist.

As she reclined in the dentist's chair, resplendent in her 1840s dress, bonnet and a curly wig, the dentist asked her, 'Are you working on anything at the moment?'

---

**FAMILIAR FACES**

'Middle age is when you've met so many people that every new person you meet reminds you of someone else.'
OGDEN NASH, POET

---

## TIME FLIES

Two old factory workers who were just one year short of
retirement were discussing their weekends one Monday
morning, and Ted couldn't help but boast to Manny about his
newfound sexual endurance.

'Three times!' gasped Manny in admiration. 'How did you
manage it?'

'Easy,' said Ted. 'I made love to my wife, and then I rolled over
and took a ten minute nap. When I woke up, I made love to her
again and took another ten-minute nap. And then I made love to
her for a third time. I tell you, I woke up this morning feeling like
a king.'

'I gotta try that,' said Manny. 'Miriam won't believe what's
happening!'

So that night, Manny made love to his wife, took a ten-minute
nap, made love to her again, took another nap, woke up and
made love to her a third time, then rolled over and fell sound
asleep. He woke up feeling like a million dollars, pulled on his
clothes and ran all the way to the factory, where he found his
boss waiting impatiently at the gates.

'What's up, boss?' asked Manny. 'I've been working for you for
over thirty years and never been late once. Surely you're not
going to hold these twenty minutes against me now, are you?'

'What twenty minutes?' growled the boss. 'Where the hell
were you on Tuesday and Wednesday?'

## FLYING VISIT

Something didn't seem quite right when an eighty-one-year-old driver pulled up outside his usual supermarket. The car park seemed to be bigger and emptier than he had remembered, and there were a lot of highly agitated people around. What was even more confusing was the sight of a huge airplane hurtling toward him.

The pensioner had mistaken the airport buildings at Palma, Majorca, for his local supermarket. He had innocently joined a convoy of official cars taking a Spanish dignitary to his plane in the mistaken belief that it was the usual supermarket car park queue.

Air traffic controllers were quickly alerted to the danger and were able to prevent the holiday jet from landing. Meanwhile ground staff wasted no time in redirecting the startled shopper to a real supermarket.

## HEDGING HER BETS

An old lady appeared in court on a charge of shoplifting.

The judge said, 'You are charged with the crime of theft. How do you plead? Are you guilty or not guilty?'

'I don't know,' replied the old lady sweetly. 'I haven't heard the evidence yet.'

## PARTIAL RECALL

Writer Hesketh Pearson and another man were waiting in a London theatre to meet with powerful theatre manager Sir Herbert Beerbohm Tree. When Sir Herbert finally arrived, he sat down between the two men and declared, 'Consider yourselves introduced, because I only remember one of your names and that wouldn't be fair to the other.'

## THE VANISHING ENEMY

While on peacekeeping operations in the tropics in the 1960s, a Royal Navy ship was supporting the British Army along a narrow stretch of water. The ship anchored for the night, and, after receiving a report from the Army that an attack was possible but unlikely, the captain ordered low-key vigilance and turned in.

At about two o'clock in the morning, the officer on watch anxiously reported seeing the silhouette of a ship – similar in size to their own – on the port side. The captain leaped from his bed and rushed to the bridge, where he confirmed that there did indeed appear to be a large mystery ship close by. He immediately pressed the alarm bell to send the crew to action stations.

No sooner had he done so than the Army post on the river bank switched off its searchlight – and the enemy ship vanished in an instant. That was when the captain realized that it was merely the shadow of his own ship that had been silhouetted against the jungle foliage.

## PERSONAL ID

A woman walked into a bank to withdraw some money. The bank clerk asked, 'Can you identify yourself?'

The woman opened her handbag, looked in a small mirror and said, 'Yup, that's definitely me.'

## LADY DIANA'S FAUX PAS

A few days before he was due to present the Duff Cooper
Memorial Prize in the presence of various luminaries (including
Cooper's socialite widow, Lady Diana), American poet Robert
Lowell suffered a nervous breakdown and was admitted to a
mental institution. Although the organizers managed to find a
replacement, Lowell discharged himself and headed for the
literary ceremony.

News of his intentions reached the ears of Lady Diana's son,
who went to warn his mother that on no account should Lowell
be given alcohol. He found his mother already chatting merrily
to Lowell, despite having no idea who he was. Greeting her son,
she cried, 'Darling, I've just been telling this gentleman how the
principal speaker has lost his marbles and been carted off to a
loony-bin!'

## ROOM SERVICE

After enjoying a couple of drinks in the hotel bar with
colleagues, a businessman retired to bed for the night, only to be
woken an hour later by a fearful pounding on the door of his
room. Through bleary eyes, he made his way unsteadily to the
door, where he was confronted by an elderly hotel porter.

The porter looked at him solicitously and inquired, 'Excuse
me, sir. Are you the gentleman who's locked out of his room?'

## CLOSE SHAVE

While undertaking a lecture tour of the United States, Mark Twain called into a barber shop for a shave. He informed the barber that it was his first visit to the town.

'You've chosen a good time to come,' said the barber.

'Why's that?' queried Twain.

'Because Mark Twain is coming here to lecture tonight. You'll probably want to go.'

'I guess so.'

'Have you bought a ticket?' continued the barber, still blissfully ignorant as to the identity of his customer.

'No, not yet.'

'Well, I understand it's sold out. So you'll have to stand.'

'Just my luck,' sighed Twain. 'I always have to stand when that fellow lectures.'

## UNEXEPECTED CALLER

Vacationing in Florida, British comedian Lee Evans decided to spring a sexy surprise on his wife Heather. While she was out, he sprawled naked on the bed of their hotel room and waited for her imminent return. Unfortunately he had forgotten that they had earlier called reception to have their TV fixed, as a result of which the first person through the door was not Mrs Evans but a rather startled TV repairman.

## NUCLEAR YORKSHIRE

A newsreader on BBC Radio Five Live mistakenly announced in 2009 that North Yorkshire – instead of North Korea – had launched a programme of illegal underground nuclear tests. The newsreader declared, 'There has been widespread condemnation of North Yorkshire's decision to carry out an underground nuclear test. The UN secretary general, Ban Ki-Moon, says he is deeply worried.'

Later a spokesman for Five Live said, 'We are aware of the occasional tensions between North and South Yorkshire, but clearly this was a slip of the tongue.'

## DEAR MILKMAN ...

It's late in the evening and we suddenly remember – probably prompted by something on TV – that we need to put a note out for the milkman. So in a tired state with our mind not exactly at its sharpest, we scribble our random instructions on a scrap of paper, ram it into the neck of the milk bottle and hope for the best. Here are some of the results:

'Please leave no milk today. When I say today, I mean tomorrow, because I wrote this note yesterday.'

'My daughter says she wants a milkshake. Do you do it before you deliver or do I have to shake the bottle?'

'Please send me a form for cheap milk for I have a baby two months old and did not know about it until a neighbour told me.'

'Please close the gate behind you because the birds keep pecking the tops off the milk.'

'No milk. Please do not leave milk at No. 14 either as he is dead until further notice.'

'Please could I have a loaf but no bread today.'

'Sorry not to have paid your bill before but my wife had a baby and I've been carrying it around in my pocket for weeks.'

'Please leave an extra pint of paralysed milk.'

'From now on please leave two pints every other day and one pint on the days in between, except Wednesdays and Saturdays when I don't want any milk.'

'When you leave the milk, please put coal on boiler, let dog out and put newspaper inside screen door. P.S. Don't leave any milk.'

## SMASHING TIME

Wanting the very best for his daughter's 1980 wedding, Grigory Romanov, the mayor of Leningrad, persuaded the city's Hermitage Museum to lend him one of the great treasures of

Russian history, Catherine the Great's china tea set, just for the occasion. All went smoothly until a senior guest got to his feet and accidentally dropped one of Catherine's cups. The other guests took this to be a signal for a toast and, in a traditional gesture of good luck, they all rose to their feet and hurled the entire service into the fireplace.

## OLE EIGHT EYES

Deteriorating eyesight is a problem for many seniors but a Chinese man came up with a novel solution by wearing three pairs of contact lenses at the same time. Since getting his first pair, Mr Liu had never even taken the lenses out of his eyes because he found it too difficult.

However, after keeping in them for nearly a year, Mr Liu began to feel his eyesight deteriorating, so he bought another pair of lenses and wore them on top of the old ones. When that failed to help, he put a pair of used contact lenses over the other two pairs, so that he was now wearing three pairs of lenses. The following day, his eyes reacted so badly to his makeshift optical treatment that he finally sought medical help, and had to have his contact lenses surgically removed.

## THE APPLICATION FORM

An elderly man called in to a bank to apply for a new savings account.

The clerk fetched the appropriate form from the drawer of a filing cabinet and said, 'Could you tell me your age, please, sir?'

The old man looked blank for a while and muttered, 'I'm sorry, I've completely forgotten. But it'll come to me if you give me a minute or two.'

He then started counting on his fingers and eventually came up with a triumphant 'Eighty-one!'

'Thanks,' said the clerk. 'And could I have your name, please?'

Again the old man looked baffled but then he started singing quietly to himself, his head bobbing from side to side for about fifteen seconds. Finally he replied, 'Ah, there it is: Bert. Bert Brown.'

By now the clerk was totally mystified by the old man's memory aids and asked, 'I hope you don't mind me asking, sir, but what were you doing when I asked you your name? You appeared to be singing to yourself.'

'I was!' replied the old man. 'I was just running through that song: "Happy birthday to you, happy birthday to you, happy birthday dear …"'

## LOCKED OUT

There are times when an outbreak of senior-momentitis leaves us so embarrassed that we just want the ground to open up and swallow us. Karen felt like that after a particularly torrid morning.

First, the washing machine had overflowed, as a result of which she was running late and nearly missed her bus into town. Then when she arrived back home a few hours later, her house keys were nowhere to be found in her handbag. In her haste to leave the house that morning, she must have left them on the kitchen table. Now she was locked out.

Trying to stay calm, she phoned the fire brigade and explained her predicament. Ten minutes later, a big red fire engine pulled up outside.

'This is my house,' Karen told the leading fireman. 'I've accidentally locked myself out. Can you smash a window or something so that I can get in?'

'Before we do anything drastic, madam,' said the fireman, 'I need proof that this is your house. Have you any documents with your name and address on? A driving licence perhaps?'

'I don't drive.'

'Passport?'

'It's inside the house.'

'What about neighbours? Can any of them vouch for you?'

'They're all out at work.'

'I see,' said the fireman. 'Well, without proof of identity, I'm reluctant to break in. You could be a burglar.'

'Do I look like a burglar?' asked Karen indignantly.

'Madam, not all burglars wear striped shirts and carry swag bags. I'm sure this is all perfectly innocent but to be on the safe side I'm going to call the police to deal with it.'

And so, twenty minutes later, a police car pulled up behind the fire engine.

'What seems to be the problem?' asked the officer.

'This is my house and I've locked myself out,' explained Karen.

'But,' added the fireman ominously, 'she has no proof of identity.'

'No driving licence?' queried the officer.

'I don't drive.'

'Passport?'

'As I told the fireman, it's inside the house.'

'Neighbours?'

'All out at work.'

'Hmm,' mused the officer, considering his next move. 'Right, madam, what we're going to do is this: we'll smash the window to gain entry and then you can show us where your passport is. And if everything is satisfactory, all you'll be left with is a bill for a new pane of glass. Is that OK?'

'Yes,' sighed Karen. 'I just want to get inside my house. I feel so stupid about locking myself out.'

The police officer smashed a side window of the house, shattering the glass, at which point Karen had a eureka moment.

'Officer!' she called out, rummaging in her handbag. 'I've just remembered there's a gas bill in my handbag with my name and address on. That's proof. Look, here it is right at the bottom. Oh, next to my house keys …'

## A TRAIL OF DISTRACTION

A 1956 article in *Time* magazine detailed the absent-minded behaviour of Hungarian-born scholar Dr Theodore von Karman, who was celebrating his seventy-fifth birthday that year. His forgetfulness was so legendary among those with whom he worked that, during the Second World War, when he served as a key adviser to the US Army Air Forces, he was followed around by a special functionary whose job it was to pick up secret documents that von Karman had left in taxis or hotel lobbies. Whenever the professor returned from a long trip, dozens of hats that he had lost would dribble back by mail over the ensuing weeks.

Von Karman had a remarkably cavalier attitude to traffic and would cross the busiest highway as if it were a quiet country lane. His absent-mindedness extended to his driving, resulting inevitably in a number of accidents. When a friend suggested that von Karman should have his car's three smashed fenders repaired, the professor answered, 'Not yet.' He was waiting until he smashed the fourth.

## TOILET BREAK

On a family outing, Great Aunt Helen asked if they could pull in to the nearest motorway service station so that she could go to the loo. After doing so, she washed her hands and then went to dry them on the machine next to the wash basin. But no matter which way she pushed and pulled the knob, the contraption refused to blow out hot air.

'This machine is useless,' she complained to another woman who was just entering the washroom. 'It doesn't work at all. I can't get any hot air to come out.'

The woman smiled obligingly.

'That's because it's a condom machine.'

## ABSENT FRIEND

Bob and Joe, two elderly friends, met in the park every day to feed the pigeons, watch the squirrels and generally put the world to rights. One day, Bob failed to turn up but Joe thought he probably just had a cold. When a week passed and there was still no sign of Bob, Joe began to get concerned, but he had no idea where Bob lived.

After a month of no-shows, Joe figured he had probably seen the last of his friend – but one day Bob suddenly reappeared in the park. Joe was delighted to see him again.

'Where have you been?' he asked.

'I've been in jail,' replied Bob.

'What on earth for?'

'Well,' said Bob, 'you know that pretty waitress at the coffee shop where I sometimes go?'

'Yes. What about her?'

'She claimed I'd sweet-talked her into sleeping with me. At eighty-eight years old, I was so proud that, when the case came to court, I pleaded guilty. The judge took one look at me and gave me thirty days for perjury.'

## TRAVEL WEARY

Disorientated as the result of a long road trip, American musician Taylor Hanson asked a fan what day of the week it was. The fan replied, 'Friday,' to which Hanson responded, 'All day?'

## TWO LEFT FEET

Fitted with a new prosthetic foot following the amputation of his right limb, Scottish pensioner Patrick Morrison was looking forward to being able to walk properly again. Even though he found himself leaning to one side with his new foot, he simply thought it was part of the settling-in process. So he was devastated to discover when the protective sock was removed five months later that the prosthetist had accidentally given him a second left foot.

## KNOCKING SOUND

A 'mature' lady from South Devon informed the *Herald Express* newspaper of a senior moment she had experienced the previous day.

It began with a mysterious noise coming from the bathroom of her house, like a constant rumble in the water pipes. After turning various taps on and off and even shutting down the mains, the sound was still there. In frustration, she called a plumber who charged a call-out fee despite being unable to discover the cause of the steady knocking.

It was not until later that evening, before going to bed, that the lady opened the bathroom cabinet and discovered that her electric toothbrush had been left switched on and was vibrating inside a glass tumbler.

## WILL POWER

An old man visited his solicitor to make a will. 'What exactly do I have to do?' he asked.

'It's perfectly straightforward,' replied the solicitor. 'Just answer a few questions and then leave it all to me.'

The old man looked worried.

'I *do* quite like you,' he said, 'but I was planning to leave some of it to my wife.'

## BLIND PANIC

Before robbing a Brighton jeweller's, a senior bandit adopted a cunning disguise, leaving off his trademark spectacles and donning a false beard. Unfortunately he had forgotten that, without his glasses, he was as blind as a bat. After snatching a tray of rings, he ran out of the shop and smacked into a parked car. Dazed and confused, he was quickly overpowered by shop staff.

## WHOSE TURN IS IT ANYWAY?

There is a suspicion – often put forward by our spouses – that our absent-mindedness might be selective. How often do we conveniently forget to do unappealing tasks – putting out the garbage on a wet night or removing hairs from the plughole – in the hope that our partner will take over instead?

American chess master George Koltanowski was a case in point. He once set a world record for blindfold chess, defeating thirty-four players simultaneously without being able to see any of the boards. Yet his wife claimed that he couldn't even remember basic things at home – like bringing back bread from the grocery store.

## THEATRE SEARCH

Partway through the second act of a Shakespeare play, a theatre usher noticed an elderly gentleman crawling on his hands and knees beneath a row of seats in the auditorium.

'Excuse me, sir, but what *are* you doing?' whispered the usher. 'Can't you see you're disturbing the people around you who are trying to watch the play?'

'I've lost my gum,' replied the old man, continuing to look under the seats.

'Listen, sir,' said the usher, 'if that's your only problem, let me offer you another stick of gum so that you can return to your seat and watch the remainder of the play. A stick of gum is not worth all this commotion.'

'You don't understand,' countered the old man. 'My false teeth are in that gum!'

# THE UMBRELLA THIEF

As the head of a large family, Richard decided to take all of the household's seven broken umbrellas to the repair store. The store owner said the umbrellas would be ready to collect in twenty-four hours, so Richard hoped that the weather stayed dry in the meantime.

The next morning, he caught the Metro to work without his trusty umbrella tucked under his arm, but as he got off he absent-mindedly picked up the umbrella belonging to the lady in the next seat.

'What do you think you're doing?' she bellowed. 'Give me back my umbrella, you thief!'

She snatched the umbrella back from him, leaving him red-faced and mumbling his apologies as he left the train.

That evening after work, Richard picked up the seven repaired umbrellas from the store. As he caught the Metro home, with the umbrellas tucked under his arm, he was horrified to see the woman from that morning's incident glaring at him across the carriage.

'Huh!' she said sourly. 'I see you had a good day!'

## FLOATED AWAY

When most of us decide that our car needs cleaning, we either do it on the driveway of our house or take it to a car wash. But Stan Caddell thought he would save money on a car wash by washing his Chevrolet in the Mississippi River instead.

So he carefully backed the car into a foot of water at Hannibal, Missouri, but no sooner had he climbed out to clean it than it floated away. Police eventually managed to retrieve the vehicle some distance downstream.

## WHO'S THE DUMMY?

Visiting Madame Tussaud's for the first time, an elderly lady was fooled by a waxwork policeman standing just inside the door, and proceeded to ask him a question. Then realizing her mistake, she said apologetically, 'I am terribly sorry. Do you know, for a moment I thought you were real!'

---

### TELEPHONE HABITS

'Why do old people pick up the phone and say their number? I know their number, I've just dialled it. Do they open their front door and say their address?'

MICHAEL MCINTYRE, COMEDIAN

---

## MY GOOD FRIEND

Eccentric Hungarian mathematician Paul Erdös was the archetypal absent-minded professor. Although he had the telephone numbers of countless mathematicians all over the world – whom he would call regardless of the time of day or night – he could never remember their names. The only one he ever called by his Christian name was Tom Trotter, whom he called 'Bill'.

His forgetfulness affected all walks of his life. In the course of a visit to the California Institute of Technology, he succeeded in losing his sweater twice in one day.

On another occasion, Erdös met a mathematician and asked him where he was from.

'Vancouver,' replied the mathematician.

'Ah, then you must know my good friend Elliot Mendelson,' said Erdös.

The mathematician replied, 'I *am* your good friend Elliot Mendelson!'

## MEDICAL ENCYCLOPEDIA

An elderly woman told the doctor that she was suffering from a whole range of illnesses, including chicken pox, bronchitis, tonsillitis, measles, shingles, rabies, swine flu and bird flu.

'Your problem,' said the doctor bluntly, 'is that you're a hypochondriac.'

'Oh, god!' exclaimed the old woman. 'Don't tell me I've got that, too!'

## FORGET THE CREMATION

It may sound far-fetched but this is apparently a true story.

A Mrs Sinclair, an eighty-year-old widow who lived on the Shetland Isles off the north coast of Scotland, was considering whether to be buried or cremated. After reading a magazine article about cremation, she thought it sounded ideal and asked her doctor whether it could be stipulated in her will that she wished to be cremated. The doctor explained that, because there were no facilities at that time in Shetland, the cremation would have to be carried out on the mainland in Aberdeen.

Mrs Sinclair thought for a moment and then said, 'In that case I won't bother. I get terribly sick on the boat.'

## BUTLER'S ABERRATION

One evening in 1921, Austen Chamberlain, the future British Foreign Secretary, attended a dinner party at the Surrey home of Mrs Ronnie Greville. As befitted such a renowned hostess as Mrs Greville, the wine flowed freely – perhaps a little too freely for her butler who, as the evening progressed, appeared somewhat the worse for wear.

Shortly after Chamberlain had begun an impassioned speech on the Irish problem, Mrs Greville became aware of the butler's erratic behaviour. Not wishing to make a scene in front of her guests, she discreetly scribbled a message and handed it to the butler. It read, 'You are drunk. Leave the room at once.'

With his mind already blurred, it was now that the butler suffered an unfortunate senior moment. Placing the message on a silver salver, he tottered around to the other side of the dinner table and, with a deep bow, respectfully presented it to Mr Chamberlain.

## WHAT'S THE PUNCHLINE?

A bishop called in to church one Sunday to listen to the sermon of a minister in his diocese. The service went smoothly, and toward the end of his sermon the minister leaned forward in the pulpit and declared, 'My brethren, I want you to know that some of the happiest days of my life have been spent in the arms of another man's wife.'

The congregation was visibly shocked until the minister added with a smile, 'I am, of course, talking about my mother.'

The bishop thought this really was a jolly good line and decided that he would incorporate it the following week in his address to the Women's Institute at the cathedral.

The cathedral was packed for the bishop's address, which was going well when, about halfway through, he calculated that the time was right to throw in the joke. So, leaning forward in the pulpit, he said, 'My sisters, I want you to know that some of the happiest days of my life have been spent in the arms of another man's wife.'

All the women were horrified. There were gasps from the audience. And the bishop stood there with a glassy stare in his eyes – his mind had gone blank. After a few moments of awkward silence, he scarcely helped matters by leaning further forward and saying, 'For the life of me I can't remember who she was!'

## CHEATS PROSPER

'The easiest way to diminish the appearance of wrinkles is to keep your glasses off when you look in the mirror.'

JOAN RIVERS, COMEDIENNE

## FEELING BLUE

Betty Vaughn was dreading telling her husband Edgar that their car had been ransacked while she was on a shopping trip in Louisville, Kentucky. The passenger-side mirror was missing, as was the garage door opener. When Edgar arrived home, the retired schoolteacher nervously showed him the damage.

Edgar walked round to the front of the car and noticed that the Transylvania University plate had also been removed.

'I can't believe anybody would take that!' exclaimed Betty. 'We've been vandalized!'

Then Edgar noticed the tyres weren't the right brand – and, perhaps more significantly, the licence plate was different. Starting to smell a rat, he checked the glove compartment and confirmed his suspicions — Betty had brought home the wrong car.

It turned out that the Vaughns' blue 1992 Toyota Camry had been parked two cars away from another man's near-identical 1993 model. Both vehicles had been left unlocked. After the respective cars had been returned to their rightful owners, Betty said, 'It could have happened to anyone.'

## BIRTHDAY HONOUR

Playing Rex Harrison's mother on an American tour of *My Fair Lady*, English actress Cathleen Nesbitt celebrated her ninetieth birthday when the production reached San Francisco. The landmark event was hailed by the media and, as Nesbitt made her first entrance, the audience awarded her a standing ovation. Thinking that it must be the curtain call for the end of the show, she gave a stately curtsey and made an instant exit.

Later when the company arrived in Los Angeles, she met Harrison in a hotel lobby.

'My dear Rex!' she gushed. 'What are you doing in California?'

## DINING OUT

For years, a husband refused to dine out because he insisted that the food wouldn't be as good as the meals his wife cooked at home. Eventually, to celebrate their golden wedding anniversary, she persuaded him to take her to a restaurant. He was so overawed by the extensive menu, however, that even after debating for twenty minutes, he still could not decide what to order.

Finally his wife suggested, 'Why don't you have what I choose?'

'What, and leave you hungry?' he said. 'No, I couldn't do that.'

## THE THOUGHTS OF SAM GOLDWYN

Hollywood mogul Sam Goldwyn was renowned for his verbal senior moments, known as 'Goldwynisms'. Although one or two may have been the work of publicists, Goldwyn's wife confirmed that she had actually heard Sam utter most of them. They include such gems as:

'I don't think anyone should write his autobiography until after he's dead.'

'That's the trouble with directors – always biting the hand that lays the golden egg.'

'If I could drop dead right now, I'd be the happiest man alive.'

'I read part of it all the way through.'

'Anyone who would go to a psychiatrist ought to have his head examined.'

When he heard that producer Jesse Lasky's second son was going to be called Bill, Goldwyn exploded, 'Why would you name him Bill? Every Tom, Dick and Harry is named Bill!'

Goldwyn once asked director Henry Koster whether he would like to work with Laurette Taylor on a movie.
'I'd love to,' replied Koster. 'She's a great actress, but she's dead.'
Goldwyn was having none of it.
'Two hours ago she was sitting where you are sitting now,' he protested, 'and I talked to her!'

To back up his story, Goldwyn called in his secretary and asked, 'What was that lady's name who was just sitting here two hours ago? The actress?'

'Loretta Young,' said the secretary.

'See!' exclaimed Goldwyn. 'What did I tell you? She's not dead!'

## HOTEL TRAP

Staying in a hotel room for the first time in a number of years, an elderly lady felt disorientated when she woke up in the morning. Everything seemed so strange, so unfamiliar. She couldn't get her bearings at all. She got dressed but, as she looked around, she started to panic that she was trapped in the room.

So she phoned reception and said, 'I can't get out of my room!'

'Why not?' asked the reception clerk. 'Have you tried the door?'

'But there are only three doors in here,' said the old lady. 'One is the bathroom, one is the closet, and one has a sign on it that says "Do Not Disturb"!'

## GRATEFULLY RECEIVED

A boy said to his school friend, 'My poor grandmother has had Alzheimer's for over seven years. It's terrible, but I guess I should be grateful for the ten dollars I get for my birthday every week.'

## WHAT'S THAT NOISE?

Mourners at a chapel of rest in Belgium were solemnly paying their last respects when a mobile phone started ringing inside the coffin. The undertaker had forgotten to remove it from the dead man's pocket.

## NOT FOR SALE

A sweet old lady walked into a shop and said, 'I'd like to buy a dead bluebottle.'

'I'm sorry,' said the shopkeeper, 'we don't sell dead bluebottles.'

'Oh,' said the old lady, a trifle confused. 'But you've got one in the window.'

## TEMPORARILY BEWILDERED

While painting Daniel Boone's portrait, artist Chester Harding asked the famous frontiersman, who was then in his eighties, whether he had ever been lost.

'No, I can't say I was ever lost,' answered Boone, 'but I was bewildered once for three days.'

## PRIVATE INVESTIGATION

Actor Hugh Grant is no stranger to being caught in embarrassing situations. While travelling through France by train, he began to experience discomfort from his first-ever haemorrhoid, which irritated him to the extent that he slipped quietly into the train's tiny washroom to investigate.

Standing on the toilet, he turned his back to the mirror, pulled his cheeks apart and put his head between his legs for a closer look. It was at that precise moment when an intruder barged in that Grant realized that, in his haste, he had forgotten to lock the door.

## CARELESS WHISPER

An elderly Catholic woman went to confession, but because she was deaf she was inclined to shout. The priest told her to speak more quietly as everyone in the church could hear what she was saying, but the woman yelled back, 'What did you say?'

So the priest told her that next time she came to confession she should write down what she wanted to say.

Sure enough, a week later the woman entered the confession box and passed a piece of paper through the grille. The priest looked at it and said, 'What's this? A packet of frozen peas, two toilet rolls, a tin of cat food. It looks like a list of groceries.'

'Oh, drat!' said the old lady. 'I must have left my sins at the store!'

## BEER AND A SHOT

Further proof that drink and senior moments don't mix comes with this tale of an off-duty police officer in New Jersey who owned a pistol-shaped cigarette lighter, which he used all night while drinking at a bar. Almost inevitably, as the evening wore on, he ended up mistaking his police revolver for the lighter – and accidentally shot a man who was seated five stools away.

---

### CLARKSON'S CODE

'There are many rules for the elderly in the Highway Code. I have one too, and here it is: get a bloody move on.'

JEREMY CLARKSON, BROADCASTER AND WRITER

---

## CREMATED CASH

When Norfolk pub landlord Martin Talbot asked his trusted barman Luke Woolston to cash up and put the takings in a safe place, he expected him to choose a secure spot. Instead Luke put the money in a switched-on oven, cooking up £1,000 in badly burnt notes. The landlord sighed, 'I thought he was joking when he said he'd put the money in the oven …'

## SAY IT WITH FLOWERS

Although he had been married to Sheila for over twenty years, Martin could never remember her birthday or their anniversary. It landed him in so much trouble that eventually he opened an account with a florist who was secretly instructed to send a bouquet of flowers to Sheila on the relevant dates with a note from 'Your loving husband'.

Sheila was thrilled by this apparent attentiveness and all went well for a few years until one day Martin came home from work, kissed her and carelessly asked, 'Nice flowers, darling. Where did you get them?'

## WALKED HOME

People accidentally leave behind all sorts of things at gas stations – petrol caps, baseball caps, wallets – but rarely their car. Yet in 2007, a sixty-three-year-old man drove into a gas station in the German city of Wuppertal, filled up his car with petrol, paid at the cash desk and then completely forgot about the vehicle and walked home. After the car had sat blocking the pump for an hour, a woman working at the station became suspicious and alerted the police. They notified the absent minded owner who came straight back to fetch his vehicle.

## AGENT'S RAGE

Ginger Rogers once complained to her agent Leland Hayward about a script she had been sent by a producer. Full of indignation, Hayward went directly to the producer's office and yelled, 'How can you insult Ginger with such trash, such drivel, such rot?!'

'Get out of here before I throw you out!' barked the producer. 'You sold us that story!'

## YOURS, IN HASTE

One of the most stressful tasks for the logically challenged can be getting local service-providers to carry out urgently needed repairs. So perhaps it's not surprising that some of the most memorable complaints were clearly written in haste:

'I am writing on behalf of my sink, which is coming away from the wall.'

'Our lavatory seat is broken in half and is now in three pieces.'

'Will you please send someone to mend the garden path. My wife tripped and fell on it yesterday and now she is pregnant.'

'I wish to report that tiles are missing from the outside toilet roof. I think it was bad wind the other night that blew them off.'

'Will you please send a man to look at my water. It is a funny colour and not fit to drink.'

'The toilet is blocked and we cannot bath the children until it is cleared.'

'I am a single woman living in a downstairs flat and would you please do something about the noise made by the man I have on top of me every night.'

'Fifty per cent of the walls are damp, fifty per cent have crumbling plaster and the rest are plain filthy.'

'Our kitchen floor is damp. We have two children and would like a third, so please send someone round to do something about it.'

'I want some repairs done to my cooker as it has backfired and burnt my knob off.'

## TURNING THE CLOCK BACK

Celebrating their golden wedding anniversary, a couple reminisced about how they first met. The husband said, 'Do you remember how, on our second date, I made love to you against the fence behind the Grand Hotel?'

'How could I possibly forget?' sighed the wife tenderly.

Then he had a naughty thought: 'How about we go back there tonight and recreate the moment for old times' sake?'

'Well, I'm game if you are,' she laughed, collecting her coat.

They parked their car behind the Grand Hotel and, with the aid of walking canes, tottered gingerly over to the fence. What they didn't realize was that they were being watched by a police officer in a patrol car.

Slowly the couple took off their clothes from the waist down and then fell into a passionate embrace against the fence. In an instant they were thrashing around wildly, their bodies bouncing back and forth, their arms and legs flailing everywhere, demonstrating more energy than most young couples. After fifteen minutes of this frenzied activity, they fell exhausted to the ground.

Concerned for their safety, the police officer went over to talk to them.

'That was quite a show you put on there!' he said. 'I've never witnessed such energetic, prolonged lovemaking from two people your age. You must have had a great life together. What's your secret?'

'There's no secret,' said the old man, gasping for breath. 'It's just that fifty years ago that damn fence wasn't electrified!'

## NOT SO DAFT

As she entered a newsagent's shop, a woman spotted an old man coming out carrying a pile of adult magazines: *Playboy*, *Penthouse*, *Mayfair*. Inside, she asked the proprietor what was going on.

'Oh, him!' laughed the proprietor. 'He comes in every week

but I reckon he must be going a bit blind because he thinks he's buying comics for his grandchildren.'

Outside, the woman caught up with the old man.

'Excuse me,' she said, 'I don't like having to tell you this, but I think the shopkeeper might be playing a cruel trick on you.'

'Oh, him!' laughed the old man. 'I've been going into that shop every week since my wife died. Believe me, lady, the joke's on him. He only charges me three dollars because the fool thinks I'm buying children's comics!'

## IN SHREDS

Gadgets are so often the bane of people's lives. One minute we're happily demonstrating the incredible suction power of the new vacuum cleaner, the next minute someone cries out, 'Where's Fluffy?'

So spare a thought for Swedish business consultant and author Ulf af Trolle, who spent thirteen long years writing a weighty tome about the country's economic future. When he finally took his 250-page manuscript to be copied, it took only a matter of seconds for his life's labour to be reduced to 50,000 strips of paper after a worker unfortunately confused the copier with the shredder.

## COSTLY MISTAKE

Having bought his wife an expensive Cashmere coat for Christmas, Joel Bahr, of Madison, Wisconsin, decided to hide it from her until Christmas Day by storing it in a trash bag. So far, so good. But then, distracted by the chore of shovelling snow from his drive, he made the fatal error of putting the bag next to the rest of the garbage – on garbage collection day. Sure enough, the luxury coat ended up in the truck along with the neighbourhood trash.

## SHOPPING ITEMS

With their daughter arriving for lunch the next day, Mavis asked her husband Eric to go to the supermarket to fetch a few items.

'What I need,' she told him, 'are two dozen eggs, a roast chicken and a knife sharpener.'

'No problem,' he said confidently.

Mavis was less sure. 'Write it down, Eric. You know what your memory's like.'

'I don't need to write it down,' he insisted. 'It's only three items – I'm not going to forgot them.'

'Well, make sure you don't,' she warned. 'Remember: two dozen eggs, a roast chicken and a knife sharpener.'

With that, Eric drove off to the supermarket. Forty minutes later he returned.

'Here are you, my love,' he said, handing her the bag of shopping. 'An egg and two dozen roast chickens.'

Her mouth dropped open in despair. 'What the …'

'I know what you're thinking. Well, you're wrong. I didn't forget the pencil sharpener.'

## AGE CONCERN

The residents of a retirement home were discussing whether men or women were most trustworthy. One man was particularly outspoken and claimed that no woman was capable of keeping a secret.

"That's not true,' said the woman in the next chair. 'I've kept my age a secret since I was twenty-one.'

'You'll let it slip some day,' said the man.

'No, I won't,' she insisted. 'When a woman has kept a secret for sixty-eight years, she can keep it forever.'

## VANISHING ACT

Nora came in from the kitchen and said to her husband, 'I don't know what's wrong with me, Bert. I think I've just had one of those senior moments that people talk about.'

'Why?' said Bert. 'What happened?'

'Well,' explained Nora. 'Only a few minutes ago I was rinsing some ice cubes – and now I can't find them!'

## THE STRANGER IN THE LIBRARY

Attending a high society dinner party in the 1920s, British actor Ernest Thesiger became so bored that he decided to explore the building. Before long, he happened upon the library, where he noticed a genial-looking man standing alone by the fireplace. As the man seemed vaguely familiar, Thesiger struck up a conversation.

'Hello,' he began. 'My name is Ernest. I'm an actor.'

'Hello, my name is George,' replied the other man. 'I'm a king.'

## FLORIDA BREAK

When an old man suddenly fell ill, his family decided to send him to Florida for two weeks' rest and recuperation by the sea. However, towards the end of the second week, the man's condition deteriorated and he died.

His body was shipped back home and his family gathered around the open coffin to pay their last respects. One of his nieces remarked, 'Doesn't he look contented, not a care in the world?'

'You're absolutely right,' said the old man's widow. 'Those two weeks in Palm Beach obviously did him the power of good.'

## NAME THAT IDIOT

During a 2004 court hearing, Australian judge Dean Mildren said he was 'absolutely staggered' that, four months previously, a serial burglar had been freed on bail for a third time after breaching a curfew.

'Who is the idiot who did that?' he raged.

It was only after his outburst that Justice Mildren was informed that he himself was the idiot in question.

## OLD FLATTERER

American statesman Henry Clay used all his powers of flattery to extricate himself from a potentially awkward senior situation. He was chatting to a distant female acquaintance when she said to him, 'You don't remember my name, do you?'

'Madam, I do not remember your name,' he confessed, bowing graciously, 'for when we last met I was certain that your beauty and accomplishments would soon cause you to change it.'

---

### SUPERHERO

'I call my grandad Spiderman. He hasn't got any super powers; he just finds it difficult getting out of the bath.'

ANON

---

## TONGUE-TWISTER

BBC sports presenter Jimmy Hill was worried about pronouncing the tongue-twisting name of former rugby international Nigel Starmer-Smith. Before going on air, he repeated the name over and over again to make sure he got it right.

On air, Jimmy pronounced the player's name perfectly, and greatly relieved, continued, 'He had seven craps as scum-half for England.'

## HOLIDAY MEMORIES

A couple were lying by their hotel pool on vacation when the wife suddenly sat bolt upright and cried out, 'Oh my god! I've just remembered I left the oven on at home!'

'Don't worry, darling,' said her husband. 'The house won't burn down. I've just remembered I left the bath running.'

## THE BEST-LAID PLANS

A man who robbed a Texas grocery store went to the trouble of concealing his face with a ski mask but forgot to remove from his breast pocket a laminated badge that bore his name, place of employment and position within the company – an oversight spotted by at least a dozen witnesses.

## SOFA SO GOOD

As heavy rain started to fall in Atlanta, Georgia, a woman feared for the state of the sofa she was carrying on her flat-bed truck. She knew that if the sofa got wet, it would be ruined. Spying a bridge over the road ahead, she decided that was the ideal place to shelter her precious cargo and resolved to aim for it, no matter what.

Unfortunately reaching the dry area beneath the bridge required her to swerve her truck violently, an action that caused twenty-four vehicles behind her to crash, resulting in eight separate accidents and putting eleven people in hospital with minor injuries.

But it wasn't all bad news: her truck wasn't hit and the sofa was fine.

## POETIC LICENCE

Poets seem particularly prone to lapses of memory. Nineteenth-century English poet Algernon Charles Swinburne was forever losing his hat. After one visit to his regular club, he called the hall porter and demanded to know where his hat was. The porter politely informed Swinburne that for once he had not lost it – he had not been wearing a hat when he arrived at the club that evening.

Sir Walter Scott suffered, too. He once praised a particular poem to the heavens, thinking it was one of Lord Byron's, when in fact he had written it himself.

Jean de La Fontaine, the celebrated French poet of the seventeenth century, was no better, as he demonstrated when calling at the house of a friend whom he had not seen for some time.

'But he died six months ago,' said the friend's housekeeper.

'Really?' replied a startled La Fontaine.

'Yes. Don't you remember?'

La Fontaine gave the matter a moment's thought before declaring, 'True! True! I recollect I went to his funeral.'

Another time, La Fontaine met his son at a social event but amazingly failed to recognize him. Told eventually who the young man was, La Fontaine replied, 'Ah, yes, I thought I had seen him somewhere ...'

## NEIGHBOURHOOD WATCH

Michael lived in a Dublin neighbourhood where most of the residents were, like him, over the age of sixty, and consequently they tended to look out for each other, paying particular attention to any strangers in the area. So one day when Michael's daughter, who was visiting, shouted upstairs to tell him that there were three men in next door's garden, he went straight to the window to investigate.

He was puzzled by what he saw.

'I can only see two,' he shouted down to his daughter.

'Two what?' she replied.

'Two men.'

'What do you mean, Dad?'

'You said there were three men in next door's garden. Where's the other one?'

'No, Dad,' sighed his daughter. 'Your hearing must be getting worse. I said there were tree fellers in next door's garden!'

## EXPENSIVE PARKING

A South African woman who went shopping without her glasses mistakenly put a 100-year-old gold coin worth more than $1,000 into a parking meter near Cape Town. The woman said she had also spent an 1890 sovereign, worth hundreds of dollars, as small change. She inherited the gold coins from her mother, but mixed them up with loose coins kept in a container and accidentally transferred them to her purse.

## FLASHES OF INSPIRATION

A couple were out driving when their car broke down. The husband asked his wife to get out and check that the hazard warning lights were working, so she walked round the back of the vehicle to take a look.

'Are they on?' he called.

She studied them for a second and replied, 'Yes, no, yes, no, yes, no, yes …'

---

### CREAKING JOINTS

'Careful grooming may take twenty years off a woman's age, but you can't fool a flight of stairs.'
MARLENE DIETRICH, ACTRESS

---

## ALL IN A LATHER

An acquaintance of Ludwig van Beethoven called on him one morning and was surprised to find him getting out of bed, his face covered in a thick layer of dried soap. The great composer explained that he had planned to shave the night before and had lathered his face accordingly – but had then forgotten to fetch the razor.

## MYSTERIOUS NOISE

A man took his car to a Chicago repair shop in the hope that the service manager could cure the strange noise the vehicle made when going around corners. The job was passed on to a mechanic with a repair order that read, 'Check for clunking sound when cornering.'

The mechanic took the car on a test drive and, sure enough, there was a heavy clunking sound whenever it turned a corner. He quickly discovered the cause of the problem, however, and returned the repair order to the service manager with a note that read, 'Removed bowling ball from trunk.'

## PLAYING THE AGE CARD

A delightful eccentric who rode a motorcycle in his eighties – sometimes accompanied by his pet parrot – actor Sir Ralph Richardson used his old age to outfox writers and directors. When appearing in a John Osborne play, he was asked about Osborne's reputation for refusing to allow lines to be cut.

'Oh, I've cut a lot,' smiled Sir Ralph. 'I just leave things out and when he comes round afterwards, before he can open his mouth I say, "Old chap, you've got to forgive me; my memory's going."'

## AWARENESS TEST

A team of paramedics was sent to examine an elderly gentleman who was reported to be confused and disorientated. They decided to take him to hospital so that further tests could be carried out. On the journey, they asked him a handful of questions in order to determine how aware he was. Raising their hands simultaneously, they asked him, 'Do you know what we're doing right now?'

The old man slowly raised his head, peered out of the ambulance window, thought for a moment and said, 'About thirty-five, maybe forty?'

## LATE BOARDERS

Three elderly men were so deep in conversation at a station that they didn't hear the guard signal the train's departure. Just as the train began to pull away, two of the men managed to scramble aboard, but the third didn't make it.

The guard came over to console him.

'Never mind,' said the guard. 'Two of you made it, and there's another train in an hour.'

'No, you don't understand,' said the man. 'They came to see *me* off.'

## MEDICAL MOMENTS

One place where we definitely need the staff to be on top of their game is hospital, but as these genuine examples illustrate, doctors are not immune to senior moments when writing out patients' medical notes:

'She is numb from her toes down.'

'The patient refused autopsy.'

'Patient has two teenage children, but no other abnormalities.'

'While in the emergency room, she was examined, X-rated and sent home.'

'She has no rigours or shaking chills, but her husband states she was very hot in bed last night.'

'On the second day the knee was better, and on the third day it disappeared.'

'The patient was to have a bowel resection. However he took a job as a stockbroker instead.'

'Patient was released to outpatient department without dressing.'

'Discharge status: Alive but without my permission.'

'The patient has no previous history of suicides.'

## SINGED SCALP

When Romanian Gheorghe Harlaucescu found that he had got head lice, he decided to kill them by massaging petrol into his hair. Inexplicably, he then chose to dry his head next to a wood-burning stove …

Remarkably enough, Harlaucescu suffered nothing worse than a badly singed scalp. The fate of the head lice is unknown.

## INCRIMINATING TAGS

Arrested for selling counterfeit designer clothing in Iowa, a Minnesota man claimed the garments were originals manufactured by Tommy Hilfiger, Nike and Ralph Lauren. Unfortunately he had forgotten to remove the 'Fruit of the Loom' tags from the clothes before selling them.

## BARGAIN BREAK

A set of Victorian military medals worth more than $2,700 was sold for a fraction of that price in 2009 after a part-time shop assistant in Norwich, England, experienced a senior moment and misread the £1,850 price tag as £18.50. The thirteen medals, which dated back to the 1890s, belonged to an antiques dealer who was on his lunch break at the time.

## SANDWICH SWAP

Two old ladies went into a café, sat at a table and ordered two cups of coffee. They then produced sandwiches from their bags and started to eat. Seeing this, the waitress went over to them and said, 'I'm sorry, but you're not allowed to eat your own sandwiches in here.'

The two old ladies looked at each other, shrugged their shoulders and exchanged sandwiches.

## LOST IN TRANSLATION

An English football fan visiting Cologne, Germany, made a careful note of the name of the street in which he had parked his car: Einbahnstrasse. When he tried to find his vehicle after the match, however, he was dismayed to discover that virtually every street in the area was called Einbahnstrasse, which means 'one-way street' in German.

---

### WORDS OF WISDOM

'The older you get, the better you get. Unless you're a banana.'
ROSE NYLUND, THE GOLDEN GIRLS

---

## SPOONER'S FINEST

The slips of tongue perpetrated by the Reverend William Spooner, one-time warden of New College, Oxford, became so eagerly anticipated that they gave rise to a whole new linguistic phenomenon, the spoonerism. Phrases attributed to him include:

'It is kisstomary to cuss the bride.'

'The Lord is a shoving leopard.'

'You have hissed all my mystery lectures.'

And in a royal toast, 'Let us raise our glasses to the queer old Dean.'

One evening, Spooner was found wandering about the streets of Greenwich in South London.

'I've been here for hours,' he complained to a passer-by. 'I had an important appointment to meet someone at the Dull Man, Greenwich, and I can't find it anywhere. The odd thing is that no one seems to have heard of it.'

When the passer-by was also unable to help, Spooner abandoned the search, returned home and relayed the account of his wasted evening to his wife.

'You fool!' she said. 'Your meeting was at the Green Man, Dulwich!'

## LIVE MISSILE

A live Second World War missile was destroyed in a controlled explosion by an army bomb squad in 2008 after a Romanian farmer was spotted using it as an anvil. The farmer had found the 122-millimetre-calibre missile in his garden a few months previously and had been using it for sharpening hoes and scythes.

## HEADLINE HORRORS

Judging by the unintentionally hilarious headlines that sometimes appear in newspapers, we must assume that sub-editors suffer from their share of senior moments. How else can you explain how the following made it into print?

**MACARTHUR FLIES BACK TO FRONT**

**DRUNK GETS NINE MONTHS IN VIOLIN CASE**

**RED TAPE HOLDS UP NEW BRIDGE**

**MAN MINUS EAR WAIVES HEARING**

**IRAQI HEAD SEEKS ARMS**

**MINERS REFUSE TO WORK AFTER DEATH**

WOMAN KICKED BY HER HUSBAND SAID TO BE GREATLY IMPROVED

GRANDMOTHER OF EIGHT MAKES HOLE IN ONE

LEGISLATOR WANTS TOUGHER DEATH PENALTY

POPE CITES DANGERS FACING THE WORLD, NAMES EIGHT CARDINALS

TWO CONVICTS EVADE NOOSE: JURY HUNG

TYPHOON RIPS THROUGH CEMETERY: HUNDREDS DEAD

DEALERS WILL HEAR CAR TALK AT NOON

STRIP CLUBS SHOCK: MAGISTRATES MAY ACT ON INDECENT SHOWS

CHEF THROWS HIS HEART INTO HELPING FEED NEEDY

MAN SHOOTS NEIGHBOUR WITH MACHETE

PANDA MATING FAILS: VETERINARIAN TAKES OVER

## LADY IN RED

An almost certainly apocryphal tale concerns George Brown, British Foreign Secretary in Harold Wilson's Labour government of the 1960s. Brown was known to be fond of a drink or three in the line of duty and this, coupled with his questionable eyesight, is said to have led to an embarrassing incident at a diplomatic reception in Peru.

Spying a vision in red across the room, Brown, already well refreshed, went over and introduced himself thus: 'Beautiful lady in red, please will you grant the British Foreign Secretary the honour of dancing this waltz with me?'

There was no reply.

So Brown tried again: 'Beautiful lady in red, please will you make my visit to your country complete by dancing this waltz with me?'

Still no reply.

Brown decided to give it one last shot: 'Oh, beautiful lady in red, the most glamorous creature in this room, I *must* dance this waltz with you!'

Finally the vision in red turned to him and said, 'I shall not dance with you, sir, for three reasons. First, because you are drunk. Second, because this is not a waltz but the Peruvian national anthem. And third, because I am not a beautiful lady in red; I am the Cardinal Bishop of Lima.'

## MAKING A SPECTACLE OF HERSELF

In her mid-seventies, Maude was starting to become forgetful but had always been grateful for having good eyesight. However when that began to fail, too, she made her first-ever appointment with an optician. Displaying the eye chart, he instructed her to read various letters with her left eye while covering her right eye, and then vice-versa. But she became so confused about what she had to do that eventually, in despair, he picked up a paper bag, made a hole in it for her to see through, covered up the appropriate eye and asked her to read the letters.

As he did this, he noticed that she suddenly looked very glum.

'Listen, madam,' he said, 'there's no need to be upset about getting glasses – especially at your age.'

'I know,' she sighed. 'It's just that I had my heart set on wire frames.'

## A YEAR EARLY

Barry and Carol Watson of Cliftonville, Kent, booked a round-the-world trip to celebrate their silver wedding anniversary, only to discover that they had miscalculated and were actually going away a year too early. Having spent two years planning the trip, they decided to go ahead with it anyway and were showered with gifts wherever they travelled, but were too embarrassed to admit they had really only been married for twenty-four years.

## MODERN TECHNOLOGY

An old man went into a hardware store and asked to buy a bath.

'Would you like one with a plug?' asked the sales assistant.

'Oh,' said the old man, looking confused, 'I didn't know they'd gone electric.'

## NEVER TOO YOUNG

During the Black Hawk War of 1832, Abraham Lincoln, serving as a captain in a company of the Illinois militia, found that even at the age of twenty-three he was not too young to suffer a senior moment. As he led his company across a field towards a gate, he suddenly realized that he had forgotten the specific command for marching through the gate.

Unable to bring it to mind, he eventually resorted to shouting, 'This company is dismissed for two minutes … and will fall in again on the other side of the gate.'

### A ROLE TOO FAR

Did you hear about the senior actress who was appearing in *The Vagina Monologues?* She dried.

## ANOTHER FOOT

An aged aunt had just finished knitting her nephew some socks. But then she received a letter from the boy's mother saying that he had grown another foot since she last saw him. So the aunt got straight to work knitting a third sock.

## FISHY TALE

A woman who was hard of hearing went to the doctor to find out whether there was any risk of her getting pregnant again.

'Mrs Brown,' smiled the doctor, 'you're seventy-eight. Although we can never rule out an act of God, if you were to have a baby it would be a miracle.'

When she arrived back home, her husband asked her what the doctor had said.

'I didn't quite catch everything,' she admitted, 'but it sounded a bit fishy. Something about an act of cod, and if I had a baby it would be a mackerel.'

---

### FAILING SIGHT

'Why on earth do people say things like, "My eyes aren't what they used to be?" So what did they used to be? Ears? Wellington boots?'
BILLY CONNOLLY, COMEDIAN

---

## IDENTICAL BAGS

It's easy to get confused over bags that look similar. How many of us have wrestled with a complete stranger at an airport baggage belt because we have insisted that the suitcase with his name, address and hotel on the label is really ours because it has the same white stripe down the side?

James Bridgewater experienced similar problems. He was

arrested in Illinois following a mix-up at the drive-in window of a bank. Police said he was carrying two white bags – one containing money to be deposited, the other containing two grams of marijuana and rolling papers. Unfortunately it seems he had put the wrong bag into the pneumatic tube.

## YOUNG BRIDE

A seventy-eight-year-old man married a girl who was nearly sixty years younger than him. As he climbed into bed with his new bride for the first time, he asked her, 'Did your mother tell you what to do on your wedding night?'

'Of course,' smiled the girl. 'She told me everything.'

'That's good,' said the old man, turning out the light, 'because I've forgotten.'

## DEAD RINGERS

A young Argentine woman who went missing following a New Year's party in 2006 turned up at her own funeral after her mother had wrongly declared her dead. Angela Saraiva had only been gone for twenty hours but her anxious mother mistakenly identified the dead body of a total stranger as being that of her daughter, and the hastily arranged funeral was underway by the time Angela reappeared.

## CLASSIC GIELGUD

Actor Sir John Gielgud was renowned for his embarrassing social gaffes, which collectively came to be known as 'Gielgoodies'. A classic of its kind occurred when the thespian knight arrived to dine at fashionable London restaurant The Ivy. As he was being shown to his table, Gielgud spotted the actor Charles Gray (who played the cat-stroking villain Blofeld in the Bond film *Diamonds Are Forever*) and veered over towards him. Having got to within a couple of yards of Gray's table, Gielgud stopped abruptly and dived off in another direction. He then thought better of it, turned back and said to Gray, 'I'm awfully sorry. I thought for a moment you were that terrible actor Charles Gray. Oh my God, you are! I do *so* apologize.'

With that, he sped off once more to his own table.

## STICKY SITUATION

Concerned that her hair was becoming a little thin, a woman decided to purchase a wig. After looking around the various products on display at the store, she eventually found one that she liked.

'How much is this wig?' she asked the sales assistant.

'One hundred and thirty dollars plus tax.'

'Forget the tax,' said the woman. 'I'll use glue.'

## PENGUIN ALERT

Passengers on a train in Germany were left stranded after the driver had what can only be described as a senior moment. He pulled the emergency stop because he mistook a giant toy penguin lying on the tracks for a dead man in a tuxedo.

## A MAN OF LETTERS

Russian composer Alexander Scriabin was notoriously absent-minded. He once turned up to a party wearing an expensive pair of new boots and left wearing two old boots that didn't even match. And he didn't even have the excuse that he was drunk. In fact, he lost so many umbrellas and gloves that eventually he told his family not to buy him anything new, but rather to give him second-hand presents.

One day, Scriabin received two letters from fellow composers – one from Nikolai Rimsky-Korsakov, the other from Anatoly Liadov – both gently mocking him for his forgetfulness. Scriabin took exception to this and set about writing lengthy replies in his defence. A week or so later he received a second letter from Liadov; enclosed was Scriabin's letter to Rimsky-Korsakov.

## BREAD FOR STAMINA

Two old men, aged eighty and eighty-six, met up in their favourite café. The younger of the two arrived by bus but the eighty-six-year-old jogged there from home – a distance of three miles. The eighty-year-old was amazed by his friend's stamina and asked him how he managed to keep so fit.

The eighty-six-year-old said: 'I eat rye bread every day. It's a proven fact that it keeps your energy levels high and also gives you tremendous stamina with the ladies.'

So on the way home the eighty-year-old called in to a baker's.

'Do you sell rye bread?' he asked.

'Yes, we do,' replied the shop assistant.

'Well, I'd like five loaves.'

'Five loaves!' she exclaimed. 'By the time you get to the fifth loaf, it'll be hard.'

'I don't believe it!' said the old man. 'Everyone knows about this stuff except me!'

## ALARM BELLS

During the 1981 World Snooker Team Cup, referee John Smyth went out one morning to buy a new battery for his travel alarm clock. He then put the clock in his jacket pocket and forgot all about it – until it returned to haunt him that afternoon. For he was officiating at a key match when the alarm went off unexpectedly, and play was halted while he fumbled in his pocket to locate the 'off' button.

### ENJOYING BAD HEALTH

'As you grow older, it's no longer a question of staying healthy. It's a question of finding a sickness you like.'

JACKIE MASON, COMEDIAN

## SPIDERGRAN

A homesick grandmother was rescued by fire crews in China in 2010 after she climbed out of a fifth-floor apartment window.

Eighty-year-old Zhang Yingfeng had been staying with her son in Hebi City, but on impulse decided she wanted to return to her own village. So she tied a rope around her waist and climbed through the window. She had intended descending all the way to the street below, but she underestimated the length of rope required and ended up dangling precariously in mid-air.

After being rescued by emergency services, she admitted, 'I thought the rope was long enough to get me down to the ground but I forgot to allow for the amount I had to wrap around my waist before climbing out.'

## REAGAN ON TOUR

Poor Ronald Reagan was often a byword for confusion. On a four-country tour of Latin America in 1982, he was given the task of proposing a toast at a dinner in Brazil. But, evidently bewildered by the schedule, he got himself in something of a muddle and said, 'Now would you join me in a toast to President Figueiredo, to the people of Bolivia – no, that's where I'm going – to the people of Brazil and to the dream of democracy and peace.'

In fact, his next port of call was not Bolivia at all, but Colombia. Even so, the visit did extend the President's knowledge. On his return to Washington, he told reporters, 'I learned a lot from my trip to Latin America. You'd be surprised. They're all individual countries.'

## FLAWED RESCUE

Perhaps one of the saddest ever senior moments was experienced by a Gloucestershire policeman who, after rescuing a cat, then accidentally killed it. Phil Groom spotted the cat at the side of the road and put it in a box on top of his car. But he then forgot all about it and drove off with the box still on his car roof. After a few yards, the box fell off and ... well, suffice to say, it wasn't a happy ending for the cat.

## GROUNDS FOR DIVORCE

A wife in her sixties called on a lawyer and told him, 'I'd like to divorce my husband.'

'On what grounds?' inquired the lawyer.

'Because he has a lousy memory,' answered the wife.

The lawyer looked puzzled.

'How is having a bad memory grounds for divorce?'

'Because,' said the wife frostily, 'whenever he sees a young woman, he forgets that he's married.'

---

### BLOOD DONOR

Old Mrs Jenkins went to the hospital to give blood.
The nurse asked her, 'What type are you?'
'I'm an outgoing cat-lover,' replied Mrs Jenkins.

---

## WHAT DID YOU SAY YOUR NAME WAS?

Forgetting your wife's name is excruciating enough at the best of times – but worse still when you have only just married her. Former child star Danny Bonaduce, who played Danny in *The Partridge Family*, met his second wife, Gretchen Hillmer, on a blind date in 1990, and in a whirlwind romance they married later that same day. The next morning he woke up next to his new bride – and had to ask her to repeat her name.

## AND WHERE DID I PUT THAT TRAIN?

If losing our car is an all-too-frequent occurrence, misplacing an entire train is presumably rather more rare. But step forward the rail driver who was navigating a thirty-six-wagon coal train from Liverpool to Shropshire in 2001. Everything went smoothly until, five miles from his destination, he was instructed to wait at signals in a queue of trains. Thinking that the delay would be lengthy, he decided to walk the one and a half miles into the centre of Telford to buy some cigarettes, but on the return journey he became hopelessly lost in a maze of shopping arcades and eventually had to phone a friend so that he could find his way back to his train. He was greeted by angry signallers, who had frantically been trying to contact him to inform him that it was safe for his locomotive to proceed.

## TOILET TALK

CNN news presenter Kyra Phillips made the elementary mistake in 2006 of forgetting to switch off her microphone when she went for a bathroom break. As a result, instead of hearing a live speech by President George W. Bush, viewers were tuned into Kyra's private chat, in which she described her husband as 'passionate' and her sister-in-law as 'a control freak'. CNN duly apologised for 'audio difficulties', but they need not have worried as most people found the washroom gossip far more illuminating than a bumbling Bush speech.

## RUDE AWAKENING

A librarian was sound asleep when his phone rang at half past three in the morning. He stumbled out of bed, picked up the phone and heard an old woman's voice on the other end of the line ask, 'What time does the library open?'

'Uh, nine o'clock,' replied the librarian, still half asleep. 'What do you think you're doing calling me at home in the middle of the night to ask me such a question?'

'Not until nine o'clock?' said the old woman wearily.

'No, not until nine o'clock,' barked the librarian. 'Why do you want to get in before nine o'clock?'

'I don't want to get in,' said the old woman. 'I want to get out!'

## UNHOLY MESSES

For some reason, the good people who compose church bulletins seem to suffer senior moments on an alarmingly regular basis. How else can you explain these offerings?

'This being Easter Sunday we will ask Mrs Fisher to come forward and lay an egg at the altar.'

'For those of you who have children and don't know it, we have a nursery downstairs.'

'Miss Charlene Mason sang "I Will Not Pass This Way Again", giving obvious pleasure to the congregation.'

'Remember in prayer the many who are sick of our church and community.'

'Eight new choir robes are currently needed, due to the additions of several new members and the deterioration of some older ones.'

'Low Self-Esteem Support Group will meet Thursday 7 to 8.30pm. Please use the back door.'

'Please place your donation in the envelope along with the deceased person you want remembered.'

'Wednesday: the ladies' liturgy society will meet. Mr Johnson will sing "Put Me In My Little Bed" accompanied by the pastor.'

'Tonight's sermon: What is hell? Come early and listen to our choir practice.'

'The ladies of the church have cast off clothing of every kind and they may be seen in the church basement on Friday afternoon.'

## SECRET OF SUCCESS

A couple who had been married for fifty-three years were asked by a friend to reveal the secret of their happy union and why nobody had ever seen them exchange a cross word.

'It's a question of education,' began the wife.

'I'm not sure I understand,' said the friend.

'Let me explain,' continued the wife. 'At college, Peter did a communications course and I studied drama. So he communicates really well and I act like I'm listening.'

## NOW WHERE DID I PARK MY CAR?

It's happened to us all. We visit a strange town, park our car in a quiet side street, do a bit of shopping and then, when it's time to go home, we can't remember where the car is. Well, it certainly happened to Eric King. On a sightseeing trip to the Suffolk town of Bury St Edmunds in 2006, Eric parked his car in a residential road and walked into the town centre. But when he went to return to the vehicle later that day, he realized that he had forgotten the name of the road and had no idea where it was. After four hours of fruitless searching, he had no option but to catch a coach back to his home in Milton Keynes, more than sixty miles away.

Over the next seven months, he returned to Bury St Edmunds ten times to search for his lost motor, losing two stone in weight pounding the streets in his quest. He finally got it back when two neighbours, who had each assumed that the car left outside their homes belonged to the other, finally realized that neither of them was the owner and contacted the local council.

## A FACE FROM THE PAST

During the making of the movie *The Greatest Show on Earth* in 1951, an elegant middle-aged woman approached producer Cecil B. DeMille and declared loudly, 'Mr DeMille, you probably don't remember me, but I was a harlot in your golden bed.'

As the crew started laughing, DeMille was left bewildered and embarrassed. Who was this woman? He could not place her at all. Then mercifully it came to him: she had been in a 1925 film of his entitled *The Golden Bed*.

## STORMY NIGHT

When an elderly couple woke up one morning, the husband asked, 'Did you hear that terrible storm last night?'

'No,' replied the wife. 'Was there thunder?'

'The worst thunder I've ever heard. I thought it was going to bring the house down.'

'Why didn't you wake me?' she snapped. 'You know I can never sleep when it thunders.'

## NEW COOKER

An old lady paid a visit to her local gas showroom.

'Excuse me, young man,' she said to the sales assistant. 'This afternoon your company installed a new gas cooker for me, but I want the old one back.'

'Surely not,' he replied, entering full sales mode. 'Your new cooker has everything you could possibly want. It has all the latest features.'

'I know,' the old lady persisted. 'It's lovely, but please can I have my old one back?'

'Madam, I quite understand that the new one must seem strange to you at the moment but it is very easy to operate. I'm sure you'll get used to it in no time at all.'

'Oh, I know it's easy to work,' she said, 'but please can I just have my old cooker back?'

The sales assistant scratched his head in bewilderment.

'I don't understand. If you think the new cooker is lovely and you know how to use it, why are you so keen to have your old one back?'

'Because,' the old lady replied, 'my dinner is inside it.'

## VANDAL ALERT

We are always warned to be vigilant, on our guard against crime, but just occasionally our crime-fighting zeal is misplaced. In 2007, for example, when an elderly customer in a bookshop in Alice Springs, Australia, spotted a man scribbling in a number of books, she thought he was a vandal defacing works of literature and immediately reported him to staff. She was suitably embarrassed when the 'vandal' turned out to be celebrated American horror author Stephen King, who had arrived unannounced for an impromptu book-signing session.

## MEMORY AIDS

Veteran actor A. E. Matthews became notoriously forgetful in his later years, so to help him remember his lines all manner of memory aids were concealed around the set. His words were written on the bases of vases he had to pick up, inside newspapers he had to read, and so on. During one play, however, his memory crucially deserted him when a telephone rang on stage and he could not remember what he had to say. Extricating himself neatly from his predicament, he turned to the young actress who was with him on stage at the time and said, 'It's for you.'

## AN AUDIENCE WITH LBJ

*New York Times* political correspondent Russell Baker – later a Pulitzer Prize-winning writer – was emerging from the Senate in 1961 when he was collared by Vice-President Lyndon Johnson.

'I've been looking for you,' said Johnson, as he ushered Baker into his office and proceeded to tell him at great length how valuable such a sympathetic journalist was to the Kennedy administration.

Without breaking off from his monologue, Johnson scribbled something on a piece of paper and buzzed for his secretary to come in. She entered, took the scrap of paper and left. A few minutes later, with Johnson still in full flow, she returned and handed the paper back to him. Johnson glanced at the paper, crumpled it up, threw it away and carried on talking.

When LBJ had eventually finished, Baker was naturally curious as to what had been on the piece of paper. He later discovered that Johnson had written: 'Who is this I'm talking to?'

## KNOCK KNOCK

'I did a gig at an old people's home. They were a tough crowd. They wouldn't respond to my knock-knock jokes until I showed them ID.'

FRANK SKINNER, COMEDIAN

## KEY CONCERNS

A senior couple were arguing about the wife's habit of leaving her car keys in the ignition.

'But if I take them out of the ignition, darling, I can never find them again,' she explained.

'That's as may be,' said the husband, 'but what happens if someone steals the car?'

'No problem,' the wife insisted. 'I keep a spare set of keys in the glove compartment.'

## TURKEY SHOOT

Roasting a turkey at home, Wisconsin police chief Richard Williams forgot that he had left his gun in the oven, one of his favourite hiding places for the weapon. As the turkey cooked, the gun went off, sending a bullet through the gas stove and into a banister in the hall. As punishment for violating his department's firearms policy, he gave himself a one-day unpaid suspension.

## THE WRONG BICYCLE

Like many academics, Arthur James, a classics tutor at England's prestigious Eton School, had a brilliant mind for his chosen subject but could be decidedly vague regarding everyday practicalities.

Upon his retirement, James moved to Devon. Cycling home one afternoon, he stopped to talk to a friend who, in the course of their conversation, complimented James on his new bicycle.

'Oh dear!' exclaimed James, looking alarmed. 'I don't have a new bicycle. I must have taken the postmaster's by mistake.'

With that, he cycled seven miles back to the Post Office, leaned the bicycle against the wall, and went inside and apologized profusely to the postmaster for his error. Relieved that his apology had been accepted, Baker came out of the Post Office, mounted the same bicycle and rode home on it.

## INCONTINENCE HELPLINE

An old man phoned the incontinence helpline and told the adviser, 'I have a problem with incontinence, but before I give you the details, I need to know that the information I give you will remain confidential.'

'Of course it will,' said the adviser. 'Now, where are you ringing from?'

'The waist down,' replied the old man.

## WHAT A GIVEAWAY!

A man in California might have got away with robbing a bank had he not suffered a senior moment at a crucial point. Having used a thumb and a finger to simulate a gun, he forgot to keep his hand in his pocket during the raid.

## LOST BALL

David was in his early seventies but he still enjoyed a round of golf. The only problem was that his eyesight had deteriorated so much that he struggled to follow the flight of the ball. As a result, each game was costing him a fortune in lost balls. Eventually his wife suggested, 'Why don't you take my brother Bill along?'

'But Bill's eighty-four,' said David, 'and he doesn't even play golf any more.'

'I know,' said the wife, 'but he's got perfect eyesight and could watch your ball for you.'

David had to admit that it sounded a reasonable idea, so he asked Bill to join him the following week. At the first hole, David took out his two-iron and sent his tee shot sailing into the distance.

'Did you see where it went?' he asked Bill.

'Sure did,' replied Bill.

'Excellent. Where is it?' asked David as they set off down the fairway.

'I forget,' said Bill.

## GRILLED SLIPPERS

When clouds of smoke triggered the fire alarms at a Hampshire retirement home in 2007, emergency crews raced to the scene, evacuated the residents and brought the blaze under control. As they cleared up, the firemen quickly found the cause of the inferno: a pair of smouldering slippers on a grill pan.

Resident Joan Hiscock sheepishly confessed that, after washing her slippers, she had decided to place them under the grill to dry. Unfortunately she then forgot all about them and they set fire to the oven. A Hampshire Fire and Rescue Service spokesman said, 'We told her it is all right to put kippers under the grill – but not slippers!'

## GIFT OF THE GAB

On holiday in the middle of nowhere, Joe walked into a local bar to find the regular drinkers howling with laughter. Every time the laughter subsided, one of the drinkers would shout out a number and set them all off again.

'Forty-two!' yelled one man, to peals of hysteria.

'Twelve!' guffawed another, barely able to get the word out.

'What is this?' Joe asked one of the locals. 'Why are these numbers so funny?'

'Well,' said the man between giggles, 'we've been telling the same jokes for so long that we've given each one a number, to save time.'

'Oh, I see,' said Joe, confused but impressed by their system. Then, plucking up the courage to join in, he shouted, 'Fifty-four!' and burst out laughing.

Silence.

'Why is nobody laughing?' he asked his new friend. 'Isn't there a fifty-four?'

'Oh, there is,' said the man. 'Fifty-four's a good'un. It's just the way you told it.'

## NO LAUGHING MATTER

Further proof that some seniors forget to engage their brain before opening their mouth was provided by esteemed playwright Alan Ayckbourn. He recalled how a member of the audience coming out of a play of his at Scarborough had said, 'Oh, Mr Ayckbourn, I haven't laughed so much since my father died!'

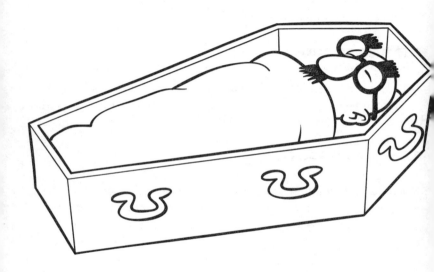

## A WILD SHOT

Hank and Steve are out hunting. Hoping to corner a deer, they separate and approach a popular feeding spot from two directions. When Hank hears a rustling in the bushes across the clearing, he leaps up and shoots three times. Overjoyed to hear an almighty roar of pain, he rushes over to the bushes – only to find that he's shot Steve by mistake.

Terrified, Hank pulls out his phone and calls 911.

'Oh, my God!' he screams into the phone when the call is answered. 'I think I've killed my friend! I shot him by mistake and now he's just lying there.'

'Sir, please calm down,' says the operator. 'I can help you but you must calm down. First things first: we need to check that he's actually dead.'

Silence, and then a shot.

'OK, done,' says Hank. 'What do I do next?'

## EASY TO FORGET

Politicians rarely linger long in the memory but UK Deputy Prime Minister Nick Clegg clearly made less impact than most when visiting a Cardiff residential home in the build-up to the 2010 general election. When eighty-five-year-old retired roofer Ken Stacey was asked by the watching media what his first impressions of Mr Clegg were, he looked a little baffled, replying, 'I haven't met him yet.'

'Yes, you have,' they said. 'You've just shaken hands with him.'

## EXPLAIN THIS

A little old lady marched into the bank and demanded to see the manager. When he eventually appeared, she told him firmly, 'You gave me lousy financial advice. You recommended that I put all my money in your bank but now your bank is in trouble!'

'What do you mean, madam?' queried the manager. 'I can assure you that this bank is extremely healthy. We're one of the biggest banks in the world. There must be some mistake.'

'Then why,' demanded the old lady, 'have you just returned one of my cheques with a note saying "No Funds"?'

## A LIFETIME OF SENIOR MOMENTS

A senior gentleman was rushed to hospital with a broken leg.

'How did this happen?' asked the nurse.

'Well,' said the man, 'during the war ...'

'The war?' laughed the nurse. 'Surely this didn't happen during the war?'

'No, no – wait,' said the man. 'During the war, I was sent away to the country to live on a farm. One day, after a hard day's work in the fields, I was clearing things up in the barn when the farmer's daughter walked in, wearing a beautiful summer dress. She asked if I needed anything, and I said no. She asked, "Are you sure you don't want anything?" and I said no. She asked, "You're sure there's nothing at all I can do for you?" and again I said no.'

'Hang on, you've lost me,' said the nurse. 'What does any of this have to do with your broken leg?'

'This morning, when I finally worked out what she meant,' explained the man, grimacing in pain, 'I fell off the roof.'

## BREAKFAST BLUNDER

The mailman arrived just as Alan was doing breakfast. It was the DVD he had ordered and he couldn't wait to put it on so that he could watch some of it while he enjoyed his toast. He might have enjoyed it more had he not, in his excitement, put the slice of bread in the DVD player and the DVD in the toaster.

## A WASTED JOURNEY

Waking up one morning, Dennis suddenly realized he was short of cash so after breakfast he walked straight to the nearest bank. But when he got there he found that it was closed.

'Damn!' he muttered to himself. 'It says it opens at nine o'clock and it's half past now. You can never rely on anything these days …'

Fortunately there was another bank across the road, so he tried there, only to find that it, too, was closed.

'This is crazy!' he grumbled. 'Why is nothing open around here? Are people just too lazy to get up and go to work? No wonder this country's going to the dogs!'

With his cash crisis still unresolved, he decided the only solution was to catch a bus into town and go to a bank there. He went to the bus stop and waited … and waited … and waited. Half an hour later, he was still waiting, his mood darkening by the minute. Eventually a woman joined him at the bus stop. He wasted no time in venting his frustration.

'These buses are supposed to run every ten minutes,' he moaned, 'but I've been here over half an hour. It's absolutely disgraceful.'

'No,' she corrected him, 'the ten-minute service is on weekdays. On Sundays they run every forty minutes.'

'So?'

'Well,' she explained, 'today's Sunday.'

'Is it?' said Dennis. 'Hell, I thought it was Monday! That explains a thing or two.'

## A BIRTHDAY SURPRISE

In preparation for his wife's fiftieth birthday, Alec telephoned his mother-in-law and asked her to bake a special cake.

'The inscription I want,' he explained, 'is: "You are not getting older, you are just getting better."'

'That's rather a lot of words,' said the old lady. 'How do you want me to arrange them?'

'Put "You are not getting older" at the top,' said Alec, 'and "You are just getting better" at the bottom.'

'Very well,' she said, writing it all down, 'I'll hunt out my recipe.'

Two weeks later, dozens of friends and family gathered for the birthday party, the centrepiece of which was the grand unveiling of the cake. As her mother brought the cake in to the kitchen, the wife was acutely embarrassed to read the inscription: 'You are not getting older at the top, you are just getting better at the bottom.'

## STUCK RECORD

A seasoned university professor had been teaching the same course at the same university for over twenty years. While he enjoyed his work, it essentially consisted of wheeling out the same lectures and classes on an annual cycle. Indeed, his monologues were so ingrained in his mind that he was perfectly capable of delivering them with his eyes closed – which is what he was doing on this particular day towards the end of the academic year.

When the sounds of stampeding students outside the theatre door indicated that his hour was up, the professor wound things up and opened his eyes – to find that not a single student was writing anything down. In fact, half of them were whispering among themselves and the other half were asleep.

'Haven't you been listening to a word I've said?' demanded the professor.

'Sorry, sir,' spluttered a student, roused out of his conversation by the sudden change in tone. 'We did listen to every word, and even wrote most of it down – last week, that is, when you first delivered that lecture.'

## MARKET RESEARCH

An elderly lady was walking through town when she was stopped by a young man with a clipboard.

'Excuse me, madam,' he said, 'We're conducting market research. Tell me, have you ever had a senior moment?'

The old lady looked thoughtful for a few moments before replying, 'Sorry, dear, what was the question again?'

'We'll put you down for a "yes",' he said as he ushered her on her way.

## GOLF LESSON

An elderly lady travelled up from the country to stay with her granddaughter and husband, whose smart suburban house backed on to a golf course. Having been on a bus for over five hours, the old lady needed to stretch her legs, and so decided to go for a short walk. When she returned, her granddaughter asked her whether she had enjoyed the fresh air.

'Yes, dear, it was very pleasant,' said the old lady, 'although I must say, there are some strange people around here.'

'How do you mean?' asked the granddaughter.

'Well, I decided to walk round to the back of your house and I found these beautiful rolling fields of lush green. The grass was really short in places – you must have cows with big appetites. Anyway, there were lots of people about, mostly men. Some of them kept shouting things at me, but I took no notice. Four men actually followed me for some time, shouting something I couldn't understand and waving big sticks. Naturally I ignored them, too.'

Holding out her hands, she went on, 'Oh, and I found a number of these strange little white balls lying on the ground, so I picked them all up and brought them home. I was hoping you could explain to me what they mean.'

## TECHNO TROUBLE

Nowadays, the easiest senior-moment traps to fall into come courtesy of that enemy of the non-young: technology. How is it possible for these modern gadgets to be so senior-unfriendly? Surely a computer is nothing more than a typewriter attached to a screen?

Spare a thought for the real-life senior woman involved in the following exchange. Faced with that perennial impasse known as 'how to copy and paste', she called her son for some expert guidance.

Son: You need to right-click on the page.

Mother: OK, done.

Son: And on the menu, click 'Copy'.

Mother: What menu?

Son: The menu that comes down when you right-click.

Mother: There is no menu.

Son: Did you right-click on the page?

Mother: Yes! I've written 'click' and nothing's happening!

## STOP SHOUTING!

Just as anyone of a certain age will remember exactly where they were when they heard that JFK had been shot or that Neil Armstrong had bounced around on the moon, anyone over the age of about thirty will remember vividly where they were when they first beheld the miracle of emailing and text-messaging.

One thirty-something in particular will certainly never forget where she was when her mother embraced the twenty-first century and sent her first text message.

'I was quite surprised when my phone buzzed and claimed I had a message from my mother. I'd bought her the phone a few years previously and she'd always claimed she was an old dog who would under no circumstances be made to learn new tricks.

'Fortunately, when I opened the message, I realized that she was still the same old mum. It just said, "I DON'T KNOW HOW TO REMOVE CAPS LOCK".'

## JETLAG

Senior readers will no doubt be delighted to learn that senior-momentitis is not a condition restricted to those of advanced years.

The following exchange was overheard by a passenger waiting in line to enter the departure gate at a London airport behind a group of backpacking students:

Security: I'm sorry, madam, you must be at the wrong gate.
Student: I'm sorry?

Security: Your boarding pass won't scan. You don't seem to be booked on this flight.

Student: Of course I'm booked on this flight. We all are.

Security: Your friends' passes are fine. Your name is not on this flight.

Student: What the hell? I booked it the same time they did. You must be mistaken.

Security: Bear with me … Oh, dear. I see what's happened. I'm afraid the mistake is yours. Your flight is at the same time tomorrow …

How the student had been issued a ticket and waved through security twenty-four hours early is a mystery – collective senior-momentitis on the part of the check-in and security teams.

## DIPLOMATIC DEBACLE

Ken and Doris, a British man and his German wife, were visiting the city of Nuremberg in Bavaria with their children. Having an interest in all things Second-World-War-related, Ken was adamant that they drive out to the vast and now-dilapidated congress grounds that had played host to Hitler's Nuremberg Rally. Having zero interest in raking up the grisly past, Doris reluctantly agreed.

For reasons best known to himself, Ken took the children up to Hitler's crumbling podium and asked Doris to nip down to the former parade ground and take a photo. Half-joking, she reminded him that under no circumstances was he to mimic a

Nazi salute, forbidden by German law since the War.

'Yes, yes,' he said, 'I'm not an idiot. Let's just take a photo and get out of here.'

Doris sighed and climbed down the steps, while Ken tried to lift the children's flagging spirits by describing the historical significance of the windswept ruin.

'And if you can imagine,' he enthused, grasping the railings with one hand, 'zeppelins parked over there, and this vast expanse' – now waving his other arm across the horizon – 'this VAST expanse ...'

'I thought I was going to faint,' Doris recalled later on, once she'd had a stiff drink. 'There I was taking a stupid photo of Hitler's podium, and my idiot of a husband standing up there doing what looked like a Nazi salute ... At least my theatrical reaction livened things up for the children.'

## WHAT A BARGAIN

When Carol came home from doing the weekly shop one Saturday, her husband was surprised to see her carrying considerably more bags than usual.

'Are you stockpiling in case of nuclear warfare?' he asked.

'No, dear,' replied Carol, visibly giddy with excitement. 'I just couldn't help myself – nearly everything was "two for the price of three"!'

## A SERIES OF SENIOR MOMENTS

When Gus showed up at work one morning sporting a black eye and a bandaged arm, his colleagues were naturally alarmed. And when he revealed that he had been the victim of a violent mugging over the weekend, they were shocked and sympathetic. They made him put his feet up, brought him endless cups of tea, and generally spent the day looking compassionately in his direction.

What Gus was too ashamed to reveal, however, was the truth behind his injuries …

Early on Saturday morning, Gus had gone onto the front step to take in the paper, and a brisk wind had slammed the door behind him. Cursing his bad luck, he rang the doorbell to alert his wife to his predicament, but she was fast asleep and didn't hear a thing. He rang the bell for a further five minutes, still to no avail.

Realizing he would be standing outside in the cold for hours if he didn't wake her, Gus decided to try calling her mobile phone, which was on the bedside table. But without his own phone on him, Plan B was made rather trickier.

Not wanting to disturb the neighbours at such an ungodly hour on a Saturday and wearing nothing but a flimsy dressing gown, Gus braced himself against the wind and marched down the road to the phone booth on the corner. He obviously had no cash on him so he called the operator and requested a reverse charges call.

'What's the number you wish to call, sir?' asked the operator.

'Erm …' stammered Gus, 'Oh dear, I don't know it off by heart. Sorry.'

Hanging up the phone and wrapping his gown tighter around

him, Gus decided to put Plan C into action. He marched back to the house, climbed ungracefully over the garden gate, and took the ladder out of his shed. He propped it up next to the bedroom window and climbed to the top.

As he was peering through the window to see if his wife was still asleep, she woke up – and, in a blind panic at the sight of a wide-eyed, dishevelled and only partially clothed man tapping on the glass, screamed and threw open the window to dislodge him.

And that was how Gus ended up being pampered by his colleagues!

## LEADING SENIOR LADY

Don't be deceived by glamour and poise: Hollywood superstars are no more immune to senior moments than the rest of us.

In 2003, *In Touch* magazine named Halle Berry Hollywood's clumsiest actor. During the course of her years in the limelight, Ms Berry has been hospitalized after a serious car accident and concussed after walking into set lights, has somehow ended up with smoke-grenade shrapnel in her eye, and even had to be rescued from a steamy scene with 007 Piers Brosnan when she began choking on a piece of fruit.

Fortunately, it would seem that the Catwoman actress really does have nine lives.

## GRAND SPEECH

Penning a movie about big business, a Columbia Pictures
screenwriter needed a grandiloquent speech for a tycoon to
make to his board of directors. He decided to use Spartacus's
empowering oration to his gladiators but producer Harry Cohn
was less than impressed.

'What the hell is this?' yelled Cohn on reading the script.

The writer attempted to explain the historical significance of
the oration, but Cohn reacted angrily.

'I don't want any of that crap!' he snarled. 'I want a speech that
every person in the audience will recognize immediately.'

'You mean like Hamlet's soliloquy?' suggested the writer.

'No! No!' screamed Cohn in frustration. 'I mean something
like, "To be or not to be".'

## WHO'S GOT THE MAP?

Former British traffic policeman William Alexander set off
to drive the fifteen miles from Hereford to Ross-on-Wye.
He and his wife were found confused thirty-six hours later,
after a 1,000-mile drive, travelling the wrong way down the
M1 motorway in Yorkshire.

## PLAYING SAFE

After suffering an injury at work, Lancashire truck driver Herbert Scott was taken to hospital, where doctors suspected a broken neck and gave him a neck brace. He misunderstood their advice, however: instead of keeping the brace on for four weeks, he kept it on for the next fourteen years.

# BIBLIOGRAPHY

Blackhall, Sue, *The World's Greatest Blunders*,
Octopus Books, London, 1994

Boller Jr., Paul F. and Davis, Ronald L., *Hollywood Anecdotes*,
Macmillan, London, 1987

Brann, Christian, *Pass the Port*,
Christian Brann Ltd, Cirencester, 1976

Brann, Christian, *Pass the Port Again*,
Christian Brann Ltd, Cirencester, 1980

Cryer, Barry, *You Won't Believe This But ...*,
Virgin Books, London, 1998

Gross, John, *The New Oxford Book of Literary Anecdotes*,
Oxford University Press, Oxford, 2006

Rees, Nigel, *The Guinness Book of Humorous Anecdotes*,
Guinness Publishing, London, 1994

Regan, Geoffrey, *The Guinness Book of Military Blunders*,
Guinness Publishing, London, 1991

Sherrin, Ned, *Great Showbiz And Theatrical Anecdotes*,
JR Books, London, 2007

## WEBSITES

www.ananova.com

www.anecdotage.com

www.capitalcentury.com

www.nytimes.com

www.reuters.com

www.salisburypost.com

www.telegraph.co.uk

www.thisissouthdevon.co.uk

www.time.com